# Small Scale Photography

## How to take great shots of your work

### Charles Lewton-Brain

Copyright 1996© Charles Lewton-Brain in United States and Canada
Drawings by Charles Lewton-Brain
Printed and bound in Canada. Video included.

ISBN 0-9698510-2-2


Canadian Cataloguing in Publication Data

Lewton-Brain, Charles, 1956-

Small Scale Photography: how to take great shots of your work!

Includes bibliographical references and index.
ISBN 0-9698510-2-2

1. Photography, Close-up. 2. Photography of handicraft. I. Title.

TR657.L49 1996  778.3'24    C96-900537-7

The author and publisher specifically disclaim any responsibility or liability for damages or injuries to persons or properties whether direct or consequential and howsoever arising as a result of any construction, design, use, application or other activity undertaken utilizing or referring to information contained in this book. There is no warranty, implied or otherwise, to the information given. Every effort has been made to ensure the accuracy of the information but any use of it is solely at the reader's risk. The author and publisher assume no responsibility for the accuracy, fitness, proper design, safety or safe use of any information, technique, tool or procedure contained herein. By reading this book you agree to the liability conditions and understand that no recourse is available regarding liability. If you do not agree to these conditions *do not* read further. Reading or utilizing the contents of the following information constitutes agreement with the above liability conditions. The jurisdiction for any remaining legal questions is defined as within the province of Alberta, Canada.


***Always have an licensed electrician check your electrical connections and use good electrical and fire safety practices.***

**Brain Press Ltd.**
Box 1624, Ste M,
Calgary, Alberta
T2P 2L7, Canada
Tel: 403-263-3955

***Dedication:*** to Erika and Aniko who make me smile when I think of them.

***Acknowledgments:***

My thanks to the team that worked with me on this project and to those whose advice contributed to this book. The team consisted of Katie Harse, Dee Fontans, Rod Stuart, and Alex Jamieson. Others whose suggestions made a difference included Dan Gordon, Bobby Hanson, Jay Robinson, Sue Archer, Georgia Deal, Layne Goldsmith, Akemi Nakano Cohn, Lyn Pflueger, Lissa Hunter, Crys Harse, Barbara Tipton, Peter Beasecker, Jim Malenda, Brad Schweiger, Elizabeth Busch, Jeff Wilkins, Henry Schlosser and Morgan B. Turney.

# Table of Contents:

# Introduction

This book is intended to introduce you to the basics of taking good quality, professional-looking photographs and slides of your small scale art and craft work. There is an emphasis on low cost and simplicity. The system as described can serve just as well for creating images of any small objects such as archaeological and mineral specimens and innumerable other kinds of objects under about three feet square (1 meter) in size. The principles can also be adapted for larger objects. The orientation of the book is towards slides and slide films but the information holds good for color print and black and white image making as well. The book is intended for beginners as well as working professionals who need quality images of objects. The book is accompanied by a video lecture on the subject and it serves to reinforce and expand upon the information given in the lecture.

This is a recipe book, about one single way to take photographs of objects which works well. It does not attempt to tell you everything, just one approach that works. Follow the directions and you should improve the quality of the studio photographs you take. As you progress you should take time to experiment with different lighting methods, begin to enlarge upon your skill and expand your repertoire of photographic options.

Professional photographers can charge up to five hundred dollars an hour. You can't afford that-I can't afford that. That's the primary reason to learn to take your own images. It's not that hard to come up with good quality shots. Even though this is a compromise system, I've had some very complimentary things said to me about the quality of the shots I take with it. I was once offered a job with a magazine ad agency in New York, taking pictures of jewelry based on the quality of my slides. So to me that's a test that says "Hey, it's okay, it's working fine, you know?"

Taking your own pictures cuts your overhead and if you have a home photo-booth then it ensures that you document what you create before it leaves your studio. This is very important in order to prosper in the field as an artist or craftsperson. The system described is also very inexpensive to construct.

I am primarily self-taught as a studio photographer and what I describe is based on my experience and what I have found works. This means that professional photographers may disagree with some of what I have to say. My suggestion is to listen both to me and to others and find what works for you. The real test is "Does it look good? Does it work for your purposes?" Try this system first and go on from there.

It is important in any project to do research. This means you should consult other photo books as well as this one to deepen your understanding of what you will be doing (for instance, if you have a camera manual read it through carefully at least three times). I suggest starting a scrapbook where you keep notes on things you notice about photographs of objects; look at magazines, catalogs and so on, try and figure out where they had the lights coming from, how the work was supported, what is in and out of focus, whether there are any things reflected that shouldn't be there and so on. Take notes on your observations. Figure out why you like certain photographs of objects that you see. One can learn a great deal just by being observant and analyzing studio photographs used in advertising images. The Kodak series of studio photography books is good because they show lighting set-ups and discuss the techniques behind various images. Sheldan Collins has an excellent book intended for professionals called *How to Photograph Works of Art,* which I recommend after you have absorbed the book you are reading now. Such books can be found in most serious camera stores. Many professionally-oriented books, however, assume that you have unlimited funds for equipment and tons of time to devote to taking pictures. A hint: it's not the fancy lighting equipment as much as it is how you *see* the object and control the lighting on it and around it.

I'll tend to repeat information I consider important throughout the text. This is because I want to make sure that you hear vital bits and pieces enough to understand what I'm talking about. So, if you notice repetitions then that is information I really want you to absorb.

**Compromise photo system**
The 'drop shadow' photo-booth that is the focus of this book is a compromise photo system. By that I mean that the idea is that it does the most for most people, is simple, is very easy to use and is rapid, but it by no means covers the field of studio photography and it by no means gives you everything that's possible. What it can give you is quality photographs inexpensively (there is of course almost no top limit to the cost of the camera and tripod). Other inexpensive options for photo systems are mentioned as well at various points in the text.

**Designed for speed of use**
So it's a compromise: it's designed for speed of use. A professional photographer may spend up to two hours setting up a studio shot - I don't think that's acceptable for most of us. We need to be able to walk in there, slam it in, take a couple of decent pictures, and then take the object away to send it off. Therefore the system as described is designed for rapid use while still giving an acceptable, high-standard result. You don't want to have to go out of your way or do unnecessary work in photographing your own objects. If a photo system is fiddly or difficult to use one will avoid using it and that misses the whole point of having one around.

Having said all that, as you learn more about photography you will see that there is a time and place for the long set-up, for taking the time to make sure that you get a truly perfect shot. This compromise system, however, gets you an 80-95% good shot fast. That is its purpose.

**Nothing leaves the studio until documented**
One of the hardest things to do when you have your own studio is to have an iron-clad rule that nothing leaves the studio unless it has been documented. This is really important as one constructs a career in the arts and crafts. The system described here allows this rule to be implemented.

**A drop shadow effect**
The photo-booth system I've designed and described in this book produces what's called a drop shadow effect. The shooting surface is lightest at the front, closest to the camera, and gets darker as it goes away and rises up behind the object being photographed. This means that you've got your object centered in the frame and the rear and upper parts of the background are dark behind the well-lit object.

**Drop shadow effect**

Figure 1

The top of the background visible behind the object is dark and the foreground in front of the object is light. The top part of the object itself is lighter in tone and stands out in contrast against the dark background and the bottom of the object is slightly darker than, and stands in contrast against, the lighter foreground which produces an acceptable, magazine-quality drop shadow effect.

We will build a kind of a 'box' (our photo-booth) that is designed to control the light that falls onto our object, which is placed on a paper shooting surface inside the 'box.'

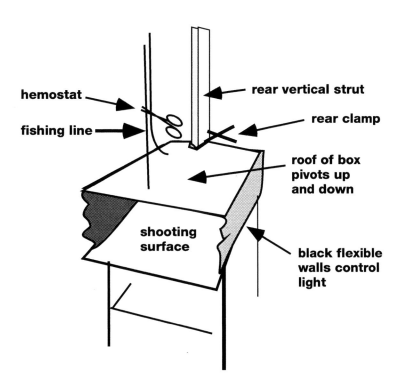

Figure 2

It is possible to set this system up in a space that is about 3' x 3' (1 meter square); the lamps are beyond that, but they can be stored elsewhere when the system is not in use, which means that it is possible to make the photo-booth part of your studio if you can find a five foot square space (about 2 meters) to do it in. Costs on the set-up for lights and the drop shadow booth construction run about sixty dollars (excepting the camera and tripod).

The photo-booth can be built on a larger scale for bigger objects; just increase all the proportions and it still works. Foam-Core® or Coroplast® for the roof works up to a point, then you have to use two layers together to avoid sagging and finally for much larger booths you would have to go to an even stiffer material like a plywood. I suspect, however, that solutions other than a photo-booth start to make more sense when your objects are over two or three feet across.

### Keep your system the same
It is very important to choose a system and live with it. By system I am primarily referring to the shooting surface, film type and light control methods you use. Choose a set of limitations and standards (the same film, the same camera, the same lights etc.) and then learn that system. One finds that when one changes a factor in the system one tends to ruin a few rolls of film before results settle down again. Examples of basic, easy-to-work-with lighting systems to choose from include:

- Daylight balanced photofloods (blue bulbs), copy stand (for daylight film, flatter work)

- Daylight balanced photofloods (blue bulbs), drop shadow system (for daylight film, 3-D and flat work)

- Tungsten bulbs, copy stand (for tungsten film, flatter work)

- Tungsten bulbs (64 ISO tungsten film), drop shadow system, (3-D and flat work). This is the option I use and recommend. Note that ISO has replaced ASA as a designation for a film speed.

I will concentrate on the last choice as it is my favorite. One may, however, note that an advantage of using daylight filters or blue bulbs is lower costs for film and the ability to use a daylight film like Kodachrome which some people prefer. An appropriate blue filter on the camera can be used with tungsten bulbs to allow one to use daylight film as well.

For simplicity and because this is an introductory text this book does not deal with flash and strobe lighting for photography. Books which deal with flash and strobe lighting methods may be found in the bibliography.

# Equipment

### Cameras
We are assuming you have a 35 mm camera. You will need a 'single lens reflex' (SLR) camera with a 'through the lens' metering system (TTL). This type of camera allows you to see through the viewfinder what will be recorded on the film. It also allows you take reflected light meter readings from your object through the camera lens. My favorite is a manual Nikon camera: I have a Nikon F2. There's also an FM2. An F3 is supposed to be good too. I think it is important to have a manual camera, because if you have a camera that's all automatic, a couple of things happen. One is that the camera lies to you (the camera thinks it sees the correct light reading for your photograph, and it is wrong) and you may end up with bad shots, and the second is that I have the impression that automatic cameras may be a little bit easier to break if you drop them, whereas with many manual cameras, you can actually drop them on the floor, and most of the time they survive - not that you want to drop them on the floor, but sometimes such things happen. If getting

an automatic camera, make sure it has a manual mode that lets you have full control over the f-stop used, time of exposure and ISO setting (some new automatics set the ISO when you load them by reading the bar code on the film canister).

Manual cameras are getting harder to find, so this means looking in the used market. You can pick up a used F2, F3 or FM2, probably for about 300 to 350 dollars if you look. Other cameras are acceptable as well. I suggest you ask a number of photographers what camera they like and why before making a decision, that is of course if you don't just get a Nikon F2 like I have. Bobby Hanson (a photographer, artist, author and blacksmith) says that many other types of cameras do not center the image properly when taking vertically-oriented (called portrait orientation) shots. You see the object centered through the viewfinder when you take the picture and when you get it back after developing it is slightly off to one side. He suggests that you look through the viewfinder and draw just inside the visible area on paper with a magic marker, thus making a frame around the edge of the view while looking through the camera. Then number each side of the drawn frame (1, 2, 3, 4). When you get the slide back, take the slide mount apart and see which edge was lost. Then mark the camera with tape or an arrow to remind you to compensate by having the object slightly off to one side whenever you want to center it in a vertical shot. I had not known about this problem and Hanson explained that a Nikon F2 centers objects properly and accurately and that was why I had never come across this particular problem.

Viewfinders may also vary in the accuracy of what you see. The Nikon F2 and F3 show you exactly what you will get, other cameras may show you slightly more or less than what you end up with; you will have to test to find out. In addition, the slide mount crops a certain amount of your image area so you will have to be aware of this in evaluating what the differences and similarities were between your experience of the image through the viewfinder and what you actually got projected on a screen at the end.

I also suggest that if you come across a second F2 body or another of the same camera body which you have that you buy it as a backup for parts. As digital cameras come on stream the manual repairs will get rather expensive and if you have a camera body to cannibalize parts from you'll be better off.

The best professional-quality photography of objects is normally done using larger format cameras than our 35 mm (small format) cameras. Large format cameras produce larger transparencies (a standard slide is a 35 mm transparency). Sizes range from a Pentax 2" x 2" (6 x 6 cm) (pleasant because the camera works similarly to a normal 35 mm camera), 4" x 5" (6 x 7 cm) and even larger. Such cameras are expensive and are generally seen as a professional's tool. Their advantage lies in the much greater quality of detail available with them. Magazines, if given a choice, will always choose a larger format transparency to work from although most will work quite happily with a 35 mm slide. If they are particularly sticky they will ask you to have a 4" x 5" transparency made of an object that you sent them a 35 mm slide of. This is pretty rare, however, and usually a 35 mm slide is acceptable for publication.

Digital cameras are coming quickly and offer more flexibility in some ways (if you have the computer to deal with them and currently primarily if you intend the images to be viewed on a computer screen). I believe, however, that slides will be around for a while yet and therefore recommend that you stick with standard film cameras for some time to come (by 2003 the digital route will make more sense). With a digital camera the additional costs of hardware and software or service center overhead are currently higher than a standard film and slide route. If you need digital images in the meantime you can have slides scanned inexpensively and saved on disc. In the system dealt with here I am trying to keep everything as inexpensive as possible and at this point digital and the resulting hardware and software requirements to deal with it are just too darned expensive.

Note that 'wet' photography (what we do now) will become an art form and of higher value with time as it becomes rarer, just as engraving, etching and lithography have done since being displaced as vehicles for commercial mass-media image production.

Keep your camera clean and dust-free. I religiously bag my camera tightly in a plastic bag clipped tight with a clothespin when I am not using it (watch out for condensation issues depending on your humidity - it is dry where I live).

### The remote shutter release and the timer

I strongly recommend the use of a remote shutter release cable. The reason for this has to do with avoiding vibration. Pressing the camera's shutter release button with a finger can cause too much vibration on a long exposure. A remote shutter release avoids this problem and only costs a few dollars.

Another way of avoiding vibration which I often use is to engage the time release lever on the camera. One cocks the shutter, pulls the timer lever down and activates it. By the time the shutter is released and the picture is taken, any vibration from handling the camera has settled down and you will be able to take an unblurred photograph.

### The lens: a 50 mm macro

The lens I recommend is a fifty millimeter macro lens. A 'macro' lens means that it blows things up (enlarges them), so you can get really close shots. Although you can obtain combination telephoto lenses that are say, 80 macro or so which allows you to use them a bit like a telescope to enlarge far-off objects and also to use them to take close-up pictures, only the 50 millimeter macro allows you to jam your head against the back of the camera body to look through the viewfinder and at the same time touch the object or manipulate the lighting on it. All of the other lenses require you to set up a tripod about three feet or further away from the object, which means that you're continually walking back and forth from the object to the camera, and you can't see what's happening through the lens while you manipulate the object's position or the lighting on it, which wears one down quickly - so, I recommend a fifty millimeter macro. Cost on a used one currently runs about $125.00 (1997).

50 mm macro lenses come 'one to two,' which means that when you are as close up as is possible with the lens, the object you are taking the picture of will be one half its real (measured) size on the film surface itself. If you have an object which is 1" across then the largest it will be on the actual slide is half an inch. What this means is that for rings and smaller objects the 'one to two' macro is near its functional limit. If you get a one to one converter for the macro lens, then you can have it the same size on the slide as it is in real life which gives you the opportunity to do more close-up work. I don't have a one to one converter, and most of the time -99 percent of the time - it's not an issue for me. For really tiny objects however you might want to invest in one.

It is important to maintain your equipment. Always have some lens cleaning tissue and the appropriate lens cleaning fluid from a camera shop around to wipe off smudges and dust. Keep equipment bagged and dust free when not in use.

There are a number of other choices for enlarging objects to obtain a reasonably good close-up of an object on a slide or photograph.

### Extension tubes

Extension tubes are tubes that go between the lens and the body of the camera which allow you to obtain close-ups. They extend the lens away from the camera and thus enlarge the image seen through them. Their major advantage is that they are cheap; the drawback is that there's a light drop off. One of the problems that we have in taking close-up pictures is that we need a lot of light in order to have more of the object in focus (see 'depth of field' later) and so any light that we lose interferes with what we're doing. There's a trade off here - cost versus the best conditions for taking close-up photographs. I had extension tubes for several years when I started taking my own photographs and they served their purpose, but there definitely came a time when they just weren't good enough for what I wanted to do.

### Close-up rings

Another option is close-up rings, which are like lenses that screw onto the front of the camera lens to allow you to enlarge objects. They come in combinations that allow you to get different degrees of enlargement. Close-up rings are also quite cheap - in fact they're a very inexpensive alternative and they may be a good way to start. Having said that, in general the more you pay for them the better the quality you will get. The problem with close-up rings is that one tends to experience distortion near the edges of the image. This may not matter to you immediately, but it may be something that you want to think about. My recommendation - if you can afford a 50 mm macro you should get one, if not then save up for one while you use your less expensive close-up rings or extension tubes.

### UV filter

It is wise to have a UV (ultraviolet light) filter screwed onto the front of your camera lens. While it does filter out ultraviolet light, its primary function for our purposes is to keep the actual lens undamaged, so that if you drop the camera, the filter gets broken, but the real lens doesn't. It also keeps dust away from the delicate lens surface inside it and when you smudge it with a greasy finger it is easier to clean than an actual lens. For all intents and purposes it's a protective device for your lens. They are quite cheap.

### Polarizing filter

A polarizing filter can be used on a camera to reduce glare from an object. Metals and certain ceramics are among candidates for polarizing filter use. I don't personally use one because I work with light placement to eliminate glare and hot spots on my object but it sounds like a reasonable idea for certain objects. The filter can be turned to various positions to eliminate various degrees of glare. Lights too can be filtered by polarizing films to reduce or even eliminate glare from an object (Collins, p 65). Polarizing filters over the lights may provide more control over specular reflections than just a camera filter (Bomback, pp 164-168). However, in my opinion some reflections are often what gives drama and life to the object. Another problem is that polarizing filters cut down on the light reaching the film and thus require longer exposures or larger f-stops which can affect the depth of field (the amount of the object in focus).

### Lens shade

It can be useful to have a lens shade for some situations to avoid flare and light spots in the lens. Dan Gordon, a photographer and educator in Calgary, explains that flare can also mean a loss of contrast and saturation even if the flare is not visible as a hot spot. Because of how our photo-booth is lit flare is not much of a problem.

### Polaroid camera backs

Most professional photographers have an interchangeable back for the camera which allows them to take Polaroid pictures using the same view they will then record on film. This allows them to check composition, shadow and contrast so that, before they commit to taking the actual picture, they will take a Polaroid shot with the camera, using the set-up exactly the way they want to do it, look at the Polaroid and make their final decision. Usually they will use black and white Polaroid film for this. There's another photographer I met who not only has a Polaroid camera back but he has a back that digitizes the image which goes over a modem so that his customers in Japan or elsewhere can see what he's doing with the shot at the same time as he is setting it up. They are able to see what the lens does on a TV screen and can make comments during the shoot. I don't currently have a Polaroid camera back - perhaps one of these days.

### Spot meters

Professional photographers use a spot meter (called an incident light meter) to decide on the camera exposure and f-stop settings to use. A spot meter is a hand-held instrument that you place on or just in front of the object that you wish to take the light meter reading of. It measures and records the amount of light falling onto it and it gives the setting combinations that one can use to take the photograph. Then you choose the f-stop on the camera you wish to use (this choice has to do with how much of the object you want in focus) and you set your camera accordingly. I don't feel that a spot meter is useful for very small objects, particularly when one has used a number of mirrors to modulate the surface of the object with small hot spots and fill reflections. I feel it is just not accurate enough. The through the lens (TTL) metering system on your SLR camera will suffice. You therefore don't need an incident light meter unless you are shooting larger objects. I don't use a spot meter for our photo-booth system. You are probably glad to read that the last few items I've described are all ones I seem to be able to do without.

### Center weighted metering (reflective metering)

Most through the lens metering (TTL) cameras are center weighted, which means that the camera light meter takes its reading from a circular area at the center of what you see through the lens. The meter reads the amount of light reflected back from the surface to the lens. Usually the metering area is somewhat larger than the focusing circle that you can see at the center of the viewfinder. As you swing the camera around to look at the object and shooting surface, the meter reading will change and with some practice you will develop a feel for where the camera is metering from. Try pointing the focusing circle at a bright spot on the object, at a dark area, and so on to get a feel for how the meter responds to lighting conditions on the object. In general you are trying for the most average choice for the lighting conditions on your object. This is why one tries to avoid extremes in lighting on an object.

Check your camera manual to see how your camera meter actually reads, whether it is center weighted, reads across the entire view or from a concentrated spot reading. How it reads will determine how you use it to take light readings from an object.

### Gray cards

Professional photographers often use a gray card to determine a reflective light meter reading. A gray card is theoretically designed to give you the average of the light that's coming back. Gray cards are available at photo stores. One can use a Color-Aid® 18% gray paper instead. You slide the gray card down, just in front of your object, preferably parallel to the plane of the film (the camera back) and take the meter reading from it with the through the lens reflective metering system.

Most of the time a gray card reading will be pretty good. Me, personally, I'm not sure how much I trust it. I tend to use the gray card every time as a check, against what I thought the meter reading should be. I will also turn to a gray card when I am unsure of what the meter reading should be.

When using one realize that if you tilt the card slightly you will change the lighting conditions coming back to the camera so, again, try for average, hold it for the quality of light you think is coming back to the camera from the object itself, generally parallel to the camera back.

Gray cards can be cut to smaller sizes for small objects. They should however fill all of the camera's view when taking a light meter reading off them.

Let's say that we didn't have a gray card around. It turns out that the palm of your hand is about the same tonal range as a gray card, so if you have nothing else, you can place the palm of your hand in front of the object instead of a gray card, and that will give you a reasonable meter reading.

**Tripods**
You've got a decent camera of some kind, and now you need a tripod.

A tripod is a piece of equipment that it is worth spending some money on. I recommend getting a used one (let your camera shop know you are looking for a good one). Bogen and Manfrotto are both good brands. I buy mine at auctions and from my local 'bargain finder' newspaper.

The photo-booth's tripod should be sturdy, heavy and easy to use. Most important: it should be designed so that when you release the legs they drop under their own weight. You do not want to have to do any resetting, fiddling around or any time-consuming messing with it. This is because there are times when your face is jammed against the back of the camera, you are looking for a particular angle and you literally stand up, looking for the angle you want, find it and then release the tripod legs. When they hit the floor you lock them in place, still with your face on the camera back looking through the viewfinder. You should therefore be able to lock and unlock the legs easily without looking at them. Sturdiness, ease of use and speed in resetting parts while in use are all advisable. Don't get too light a tripod; because it is for a studio situation stability is more important than portability.

Note that in practice one rarely tries to use the central vertical pillar of a tripod upon which the camera is mounted. While it may extend upwards with a crank and it seems like an easy way to raise the camera's position it can shake more than if one uses the tripod's legs to do so. Because exposure times tend to be long with close-up work this shake can result in poor images. If your photo system is in a basement on a solid floor this is less of a problem but passing trucks and floor vibration can still cause problems. One might as well minimize it by not extending the central pillar upwards more than necessary.

It is also a good idea to have a tripod that has a central pillar which allows one to mount the camera on the bottom of the pillar as well as the top. This allows you to place the camera on the bottom of the pillar between the tripod's legs, facing down, in order to use the tripod as a copy stand for flat work. Note that I personally do not use this much; it is just an option that it can be nice to have at times.

A ball head design is generally not as accurate to use for positioning as one that hinges and tilts in several directions.

Sometimes one sets a tripod up so that the two legs at the front are fairly short and the third leg is out all the way extended backwards. This is to allow the camera to look down almost vertically for certain shots. To stabilize it you may want a sand bag at the end of the extended leg. I like to buy an old leather hand bag with a zipper for a dollar or so at a thrift store, fill a plastic shopping bag with sand, tie it up and zip it into the hand bag. This gives you a sand bag with handles that you can easily move about and if necessary hang from something to keep it steady. It can be useful to have more than one of these around.

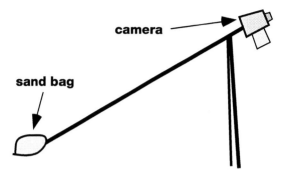

Figure 3

This tip is really important: when you mount the camera onto the tripod head make sure that the rewind release button on the bottom of the camera is exposed, that you can still get at it when the camera is mounted on the head; otherwise you have to move the camera to unload and load film. While it may seem incredibly obvious to some people, this simple camera positioning took me years to figure out.

### 64 ISO tungsten film

The film that I'm going to recommend, and that I use myself, is 64 ISO Tungsten Ecktachrome film. It only comes in 36-shot rolls. It is used with photoflood bulbs. Even though it says 64 ISO on the box, in actual practice you set the ISO on the camera to 50 (check the instructions that come with the film). You can happily use Tungsten Fujichrome film, and other brands as well, but I tend to prefer the Kodak Ektachrome, simply because it's what I'm used to. Fujichrome is however quite acceptable, works great, and seems to be similar. You should find the letter 'T' next to the film ISO on tungsten film. It is worth checking for this as I've seen more than one person blow a roll of film of their objects by getting daylight film because they didn't check for the 'T' on the box of film they bought. Always buy more than one roll of film - you don't want to be stuck needing one at a critical moment.

Professional films come out of a refrigerator at the photo shop and are stored in one before and after use. I always buy in bulk packs of twenty and get a hefty discount because of it. If you buy film with the same emulsion batch number (usually the case when buying twenty at once) you can be assured of consistency in color amongst them as there are slight differences in color in every emulsion batch produced. As long as it is in a refrigerator the film can be stored almost indefinitely. Some photographers store film in the freezer compartment of their refrigerator.

With the Tungsten Ecktachrome film that I recommend, there is a tendency to render blues and greens quite well and reds come out pretty well. The Fuji films tend to have a little bit more of a bias towards the blue and the green, so if your work has a lot of blue and green in it, perhaps you wish to consider Fuji. Again, choose a film type and try and live with it. If they are having slides reproduced in a magazine some photographers will take a slide of a Kodak Color Patch Strip (available from photo suppliers) at the same time as they shoot the objects. This slide is sent in with the slides for reproduction and can help the printer (if they bother) to better match the actual colors of the work (Meltzer, p 48).

***Important: set your camera to 50 ISO with the 64T ISO film and photofloods***

## Kodachrome slide film

Some professionals use Kodachrome film. Kodachrome is a daylight film, and it has to be processed by Kodak approved labs, which means that you can't shoot a roll of Kodachrome film and have it this afternoon like you can with the other slide films: it must be mailed off for processing. With Kodachrome the advantage is that it gives you warmer tones in the reds and in the pinks, so some professionals prefer Kodachrome, particularly for the flesh tones in shooting people, which in my case, because I'm shooting jewelry and craft objects, is not an issue. If the objects you are shooting have a lot of reds and yellows in them you might try it out. If you use Kodachrome film for the drop shadow photo system you will have to use the daylight balanced photofloods (blue bulbs) or the appropriate filter to modify the tungsten lighting.

According to Collins, Kodachrome also has the best dye stability of any film (as long as it is stored in the dark) but fades faster than any of them upon projection, requiring duplicates for actual projection use. Meltzer prefers Kodachrome 25 or 64 over other film types for shooting craft objects (Meltzer, p 25).

## 160 ISO tungsten film

Many professionals will use 160 ISO Tungsten Ecktachrome film for studio work. The reason that they do this is because they're shooting people, and people move and breathe and walk around, so they need to have a faster shutter speed in order not to have blurred pictures, but with our system we're shooting immobile jewelry, ceramics or other small objects so we don't have to worry about having to use a fast shutter speed. I also believe that we get better results, better grain and better control over our depth of field by choosing a lower ISO film, such as the ISO 64 film, than we'd ever get with the ISO 160 film. I have had troubles when using the ISO 160 - a result I think of being used to the ISO 64 because I've seen great results from professionals who only use the ISO 160 even when shooting craft objects. Again, a chosen fixed film type lets you learn it and control the results. If you want to learn with the ISO 160T it is in general slightly more available than the ISO 64T.

## Let the film warm up for 15 minutes

The films we use (for example the 64 ISO Tungsten Ecktachrome) should be stored in a refrigerator until use. Take it out a good fifteen minutes before use so it warms up slowly; this avoids condensation problems. After you have shot the roll put it back into a fridge until you get around to having it processed. I keep all my films in a refrigerator to avoid them 'maturing.' Watch out for putting film onto a radiator or allowing it to get hot by accident - heat can really wreck film.

## Black and white film

Black and white film is another thing to consider and at this point I would recommend TMax ISO 400 film, just for your general purpose black and white photographs. I've also used Kodak Plus-X. Kodak Technical Pan film is recommended by Collins. Another film that I've used a fair bit recently is Ilford XP2. The main advantage of Ilford XP2 is that it can be processed in any one-hour photo machine, using what's called the C 41 color print process, and this means that you can shoot a roll of black and white film and have the negatives back very quickly, which is an advantage when compared with having standard black and white done commercially. If you want prints done on a standard one-hour color printing machine this is not a problem, but you have to tell the photo shop to use the correct black and white paper to print on, as otherwise you will get a yellowish or bluish toned image - which may have a certain charm but is usually not useful for PR purposes which is generally the point of making black and white prints.

Many quick-print photo shops send out to do the black and white printing even on a color printing machine so you may have to ask around a bit to find a place whose service suits your needs in terms of time and cost. If a shop has the special black and white paper on hand it can be anywhere from hours to several days to get the black and white prints back.

I believe the best route for black and white printing is to print it yourself. It is not that hard to do, is the least costly option and offers the most control of your results. You can learn how to do adequate black and white prints in an afternoon from a photographer with a darkroom. Essentials include a good enlarger, the use of test strips and probably RC (rapid) photo paper, not too contrasty. Once the XP2 negatives have been processed they can be printed like any normal black and white film negative. It is usually possible to find a darkroom to borrow once or twice a year and then print like mad (at least 8 of each print is useful for PR reasons). If you can't borrow access most cities have a darkroom rental service for a reasonable cost if you are going in with a plan to test strip and batch print rapidly. The ability to manipulate things in the darkroom can to some extent compensate for errors in image making and allow some flexibility in contrast control.

For printing for reproduction I like Polycontrast glossy RC paper, printed at a contrast level of 2 or 3. A batch printing procedure for beginners is described in the appendices.

Magazines do not, in my experience, print color shots of one's work unless one is quite famous; they print black and white, so it's really important to know how to do black and white photography. The nice thing about taking black and white photographs is you don't have to use any fancy lighting; anything counts, anything at all - desk lamps, it doesn't matter, anything. The hard part is that it's really hard to see tone, contrast and so on in terms of black and white when what your eyes are used to seeing is color. Being able to do this is a matter of practice and is tricky. You've got to watch contrast when you're shooting black and white; you have to make sure the lighting is very, very even, and tonally average, of course with some slight amount of deep blacks and white whites. As always watch out for hot spots (too bright an area on the object).

Black and white film can be used to copy from slides to obtain black and white prints of color slides that you like. You can project a slide onto a white wall or card, set up the camera as close a possible to parallel and centered on the projected image and take the shot. If the red areas come out too light and the blue too dark consider experimenting with a filter like a Wratten 82A (Meltzer, p 100). One can shoot black and white film on a slide duplicator for a similar effect. Jeff Wilkins, a Calgary artist, suggests using a new black and white transparency film called Scala 200 for black and white slides for magazines to work from.

### Color print film
Some people will use the daylight filter, or daylight bulbs, and shoot daylight film prints of their objects: color prints. The reason for this is so that they can have them in a portfolio, so they can get reprints made and pass them out and send them on. Are they useful? Magazines aren't going to use them, but if you have a color print, you can then use a copy stand and make a slide off that. So for some people that's their route; they do all color prints, and if they need slides, they shoot slides of the prints. Note that color print negatives are apparently even less stable than color transparency (slide) films over the long haul. Color prints can be a positive part of a presentation to a client or a gallery but unless larger than 4" x 6" they feel a little like a 'snapshot' (not a high-status reference), so if using them in presentations change the context and references for the viewer and print them at 8" x 10" which is definitely more impressive.

You can also buy special films from Los Angeles which are often advertised in the backs of photography magazines which are actually movie film. It is 35 millimeter film; it's very high-detail and is interesting because the same film can be used to make prints or slides, both, and that has advantages for some people. I didn't like it personally when I tried it; but some people swear by it.

One of the other things about color prints is that, providing you either know how to print them yourself or are willing to pay someone, there is some possible flexibility and control of the final image available.

I don't personally use color prints much; I stick to color slides and if I need a print then I have one made from the slide. Ilfochrome (Cibachrome) (a direct print from the slide) gave me my best results but it is getting harder to find this process now. Your camera shop may just shoot an internegative of your slide onto color print film and then print it (that is, they take a color print photo of your slide). Ask them what your best route for quality is and what options are available to you. Very good laser photocopies from slides are available and quality can go from reasonable for the cost to an expensive, almost perfect reproduction of the image. There tends to be an increase in image contrast in most reproduction and printing methods.

Where color prints make sense is in portfolios. Crys Harse reports that when she approached German galleries for an exhibition she had to have her slides made into color prints before they would deal with her.

### Lights (photofloods)
The kind of lights and lighting that I recommend for our drop shadow system are photofloods (type B). You can buy these bulbs at many photo stores but you should shop around: prices vary from 2 dollars to 10 dollars per bulb. They are a pretty standard item in photo stores that sell to professionals. Tell the camera store staff you will be using tungsten film.

They are mounted in clamp-on lights, such as you might find at a hardware store, where there's a spun aluminum bell and a little clamp-on part to the light socket. The best quality ones have ceramic sockets, so you should try and find ones with ceramic sockets if at all possible. The plastic socket kind can overheat, their switches tend to wear out and they are usually not rated for the high wattage used in photoflood bulbs - which makes them both dangerous and probably illegal in the event of a fire.

We will use three main light sources for our system: two 250 watt bulbs and one 500 watt bulb. The 500 watt one is above the shooting surface and the 250 watt ones are above and on the sides. I recommend buying at least four of the 250 watt bulbs and three of the 500 watt bulbs and having that many on hand most of the time. It can be very frustrating to burn out your last bulb in the middle of an important photo shoot and not have a replacement on hand. We will be using three lights for our system and that will serve us very well most of the time. When you handle and change the bulbs use a clean cloth like a handkerchief or cotton gloves like they sell in camera stores. Grease traces on the bulb can apparently sometimes contribute to bulb failure (note that if you ever change halogen slide projector bulbs you should treat them the same way).

Remember to shut off any other sources of light when you are shooting as incandescent bulbs or fluorescent bulbs nearby can affect the colors you get in your photographs. Tungsten films do not react well to other types of lights being on at the same time when you take photographs with them.

The photoflood bulbs in the clamp-on lights are used most of the time with light diffusion screening such as Mylar® between them and the object being photographed. Mirrors are used to collect light from the photofloods and so add light to different parts of the object. Diffusers have been omitted in the following drawing for clarity.

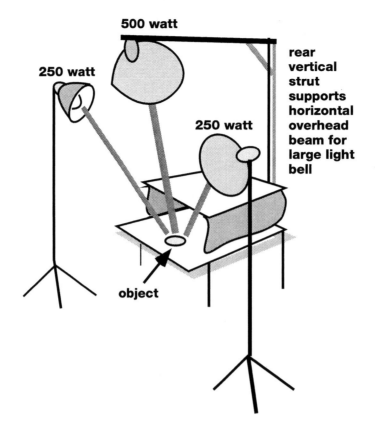

**500 watt**

**250 watt**

**250 watt**

rear
vertical
strut
supports
horizontal
overhead
beam for
large light
bell

object

Figure 4

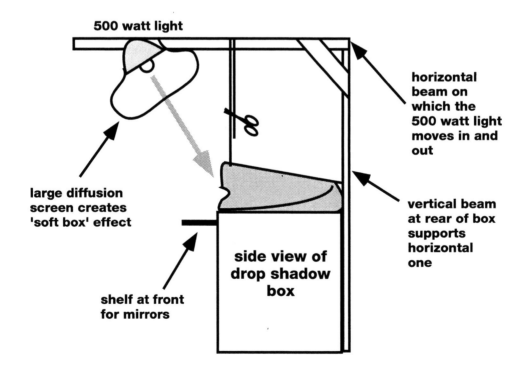

**500 watt light**

horizontal
beam on
which the
500 watt light
moves in and
out

large diffusion
screen creates
'soft box' effect

vertical beam
at rear of box
supports
horizontal
one

**side view of
drop shadow
box**

shelf at front
for mirrors

Figure 5

## Light dimmer box: ramping the lights up and down

The light bulbs and your entire lighting system should, if possible, be run through a light dimmer box. You can buy a light dimmer at the hardware store and construct a box, or get an electrician friend to do this for you. Remember that the dimmer box should be rated for the wattage you will run through it to avoid any fire danger. The reason for having a dimmer box is that we want to ramp the lights up and down. In my experience it is when you turn the lights on that you blow the bulbs. One therefore tries not to turn them on suddenly. If you ramp the lights up and down, you'll find they last a lot longer, and it's a lot gentler on them. In addition you want, if possible, to turn the lights on and off from a single place to make life easier. The dimmer box should be wired to plugs for the lights. If you use the on/off switches on the clamp-on lights themselves, they often break after a period of time, so anything you can do to displace that switching as well as the on/off shock to the bulbs is beneficial.

## Log book

A point about photofloods and professionals: professional photographers will keep a logbook of their photoflood use, and they will note every minute of running time, and when that bulb hits 2 hours they scrap the bulbs, even if the bulbs are still functioning. Now after a lot of experience, I don't feel this is necessary. I feel that if you start off with three photoflood bulbs and you just use them, after a little while you have one old, one new, and one medium, there is a blend of light qualities and it all works out. I have yet to see any disturbance in color temperature from not keeping a log book and not trashing my bulbs every few hours. I use the bulbs until they die and then change them. This lowers your overhead. A professional photographer told me once that when bulbs are tested more sensitive films than normal are used and so in real life it doesn't make as much difference as one might think.

While not a log book as such I strongly recommend keeping a note book and pen next to your shooting area to note your observations and experiences in. This will help you better understand what you are doing and help keep you out of trouble when similar problem situations crop up more than once.

## Mirrors

A major part of our system, and what makes it an extremely good one, is the use of mirrors. I like swiveling shaving mirrors which cost two or three dollars each. You can also use the kind of make-up mirror that enlarges things on one side and on the other there is a regular reflection. Make sure that the rim on the mirror is silvery or white as colored rims can reflect in your work. These kinds of mirrors are very useful for our purposes. I have some 15 to 20 mirrors in various sizes around my own set-up. The photofloods and mirrors will be all you need in lighting equipment to obtain good results. Mirrors used should be stable and easy to tilt and position. They should also not move after you position them. The mirrors catch hard light falling from the sides of the clamp-on lights and give us miniature spotlights on the object. It is the mirrors that allow us to model light on the object and obtain results equal to or better than those available with professional photographic lighting equipment costing thousands of dollars.

This is all antique technology. This is how they made the original 1920s *The Hunchback of Notre Dame;* they used mirrors to shine the light, and it's something that photographers these days have forgotten about to some extent, but it's extremely useful, particularly for the small scale objects that we'll be shooting.

I often use the mirrors in ranked layers, one behind and perhaps above the next so both can be used. I also have mirrors that drop down from the ceiling; I have mirrors everywhere I can put them. I like microscope mirrors too, small ones which I then mount so that they can swivel. You can buy them at a flea market, and these can sit right on the shooting surface to direct light onto your object.

Several additional options that can sometimes be useful follow.

### Projectors
A source of light that I sometimes use for my photo-booth is slide projectors. Slide projectors have the correct color temperature light for the type of film that we'll be using. If you go to a flea market you can buy a functional older slide projector for 5 or 6 dollars - often they are the type of slide projectors that have the slides organized in a long rectangular tray. They're such a pain to use that people are happy to get rid of them and they're very cheap. When one considers that the bulbs alone used to run about $25.00 each it is a pretty good deal. So, if you can buy a slide projector inexpensively, mount it onto some kind of tripod, then that too becomes a light for our system. One can mask parts of the lens with dark paper to create 'stripes' of light. Occasionally a slide projector provides a great 'feed' of hard light to a mirror or may be bounced off a white surface onto an object as a 'fill' light to illuminate a dark portion of a piece.

### Quartz-halogen work lamps
There are now quartz-halogen 'work lamps' available at hardware stores for between fifteen and thirty-five dollars which gives you a photo lamp that several years ago a photographer would pay three or four hundred dollars for. They have more or less the same color temperature as photofloods. They tend to be rather bright though and I don't use them for the small scale system we are talking about, more for larger objects outside of the photo-booth or for shots of rooms. For larger objects however they can be a very cost-effective addition to photographic lighting for tungsten films.

### Daylight balanced photofloods (blue bulbs)
An option that some people use for photography instead of the tungsten photofloods is daylight balanced photofloods, often called 'blue bulbs.' These are bulbs intended for daylight film types rather than the tungsten film that I recommend. The main advantage here is cost: the tungsten film costs more than daylight film. However, blue bulbs (and blue filters) cut down on the amount of light that reaches the film and this may affect the capabilities of your system. Again, choose a system, learn it and live with it.

### Blue filters
Instead of using the blue bulbs, it is also possible to use a blue filter on your camera lens, which allows you to use tungsten lighting with daylight film. Some people really like the option of being able to use daylight film. This is a pretty inexpensive way of having the flexibility of both options with your photo system. I don't have one and it is not something that I do because I like to stick to a single film type to avoid surprises, but it may be useful for you to know about at some point. At the photo shop ask for the filter that allows you to shoot daylight film using tungsten photoflood (3200K) bulbs. In the Kodak Wratten system this would be an 80A correction filter. This requires an exposure increase of about two f-stops (Collins, p 64).

The reason some people like the daylight film option (besides the ability to use Kodachrome) is because they prefer to shoot color print film of their work which can be processed rapidly almost anywhere and is relatively inexpensive. In practice I personally don't find color prints that useful when compared with slides.

If I need to have color prints then slides can be easily duplicated onto color print film. As well, good prints can be made from slides at most photo shops and there is always the option of having a laser-scanned color photocopy made from a slide. If on the other hand you do have color prints you want slides of you can get fairly good results by taking slides of the color prints themselves using the principles of a horizontal copy set-up (described later).

### Fiber-optic lights

If you have an extra couple of hundred dollars around I strongly recommend obtaining one or two fiber optic light sources as well. They can be purchased from gemology suppliers. They provide several settings of a tungsten-halogen intense spotlight on a long gooseneck that can be twisted and positioned fairly close to a small object. The end of the 'light pipe' or gooseneck is about 1/2" across. They are very pleasant to have around and enable some really accurate spotlighting and elimination of shadows on a piece. I don't have one of my own but I use them whenever I have them available.

# My Recommended Lighting Pick for Beginners:

Until you have some experience I suggest my recipe for basic success: 3 photoflood bulbs, one large one above, two of less wattage on the sides, diffusion screens on all of them and use 64 ISO tungsten film (don't bother using blue bulbs, daylight film etc. for a bit). This is what I use.

Again, whatever you do, set up a strict system, and live with it, and that way you'll get the best results.

# Photo-Booth Systems

### Using a copy stand

A vertical copy stand is sometimes used for shooting prints, drawings, jewelry and other fairly flat objects. A copy stand is designed so that one has vertical movement of the camera while it faces down. There are usually fixed lights at 45 degree angles to the shooting surface. The vertical column that the camera is mounted on keeps the plane of the film parallel to the shooting surface which gives good results for very flat objects like prints, drawings and documents. A small bubble level to place on the back of the camera is useful to ensure that your film plane is in the same plane as the flat art being copied. If using a copy stand for low-relief and three-dimensional work remember that diffuse light is important in object photography and consider using diffusion screens over your lights.

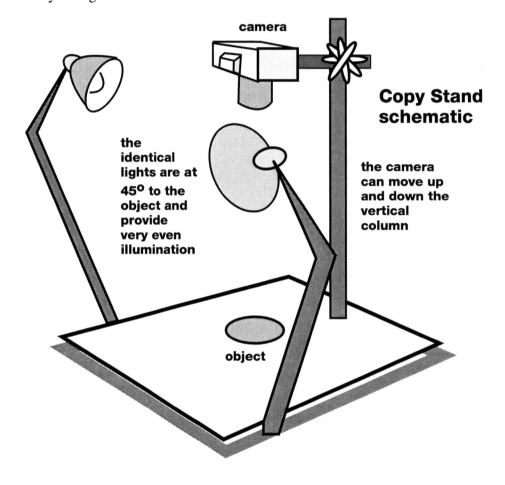

**camera**

**Copy Stand schematic**

the identical lights are at 45° to the object and provide very even illumination

the camera can move up and down the vertical column

**object**

Figure 6

While a copy stand can be useful, the drop shadow system we're building is more flexible as it allows us to take photographs of both flat things and three-dimensional objects. However, if you have a lot of work or objects that are really flat, perhaps a copy stand would be a good way to go.

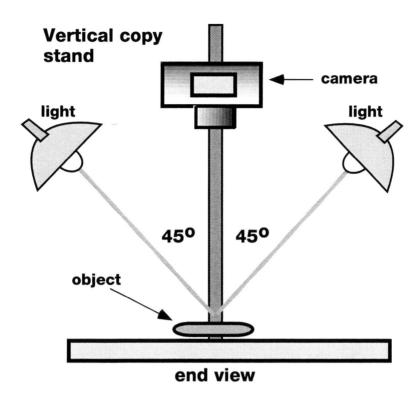

Figure 6.1

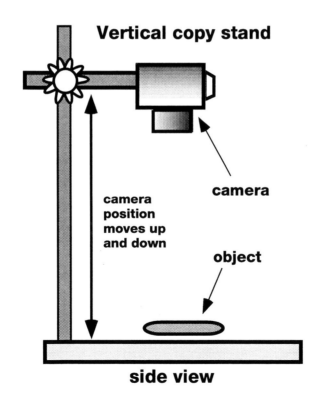

Figure 6.2

Horizontal copy sets are used for flat art that can hang on a wall. This basically consists of hanging the flat art on a wall and positioning the camera and lights carefully to provide very even lighting with the camera exactly centered, level and its back parallel to the flat artwork. Often one lays out tape on the wall and floor to define a central axis line for the camera and artwork. The camera is also centered vertically on the artwork (it's as close to the middle of the artwork as possible). Collins suggests painting the surrounding wall gray or black to help reduce glare in the image. Very even lighting with the pool of uniform light about 20% larger than the artwork is beneficial (Collins, pp 139, 140). Be aware of glare, surface texture, edges and brightness as you check your image before taking the shot. A level can be useful for both camera and artwork.

**A professional's drop shadow box**
To produce a drop shadow effect, a professional photographer might use a very long wooden framework like a long rectangular crate frame, perhaps 8 to 12 feet long, and they would place the object at the front of this construction. Inside this, they might have a long piece of seamless paper that rises very gently from the front of this long rectangular space all the way to the back. The top would be covered by a diffusion Mylar® or its equivalent. It produces a wonderful drop shadow effect, but if you're like me, you don't have a lot of room in your studio, so such a construction is out of the question. Our compromise photo-booth system is designed to operate in a much smaller space.

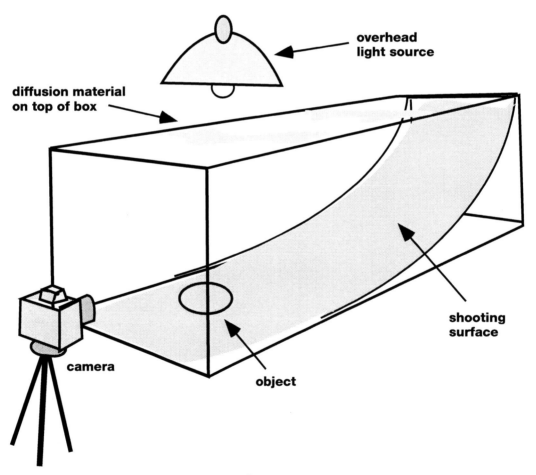

Figure 7

Another version professionals use on a table top is to have a seamless paper background, often white or light gray, and they obtain the drop shadow effect by having the lights directed onto the object at the front of the shooting surface, leaving the upper rear portions of the seamless paper in darkness while the camera light meter reading is correctly set for the well-lit object at the front (see figure 8). Professionals also use 'gobos,' that is, black cardboard shapes cut and held by stands in such a way as to block and subtract light falling behind the object, thus enhancing the drop shadow effect.

A method which I like is to use a piece of seamless shooting surface paper which actually darkens smoothly from white or a light gray at the front to dark, almost black at the top. This does a pretty good job of producing a drop shadow effect behind an object placed at the front of the shooting surface. Such paper shooting surfaces can be bought commercially or, as I do, made by using a very light, fine spatter of gray or black spray paint to progressively darken one end of the sheet of paper.

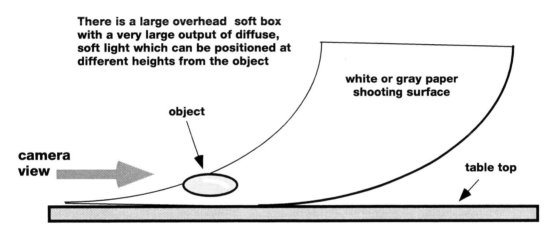

Professionals tabletop set-up. The lights are arranged to light the object from above and to leave the rear section of the shooting surface paper in relative darkness thus producing a drop shadow effect.

Figure 8

A large overhead diffuser (a soft box) is a very important lighting option for many objects, (ceramics is an example) and with appropriate use of fill cards (white reflectors to lighten areas too dark on the object) it can be an excellent solution for documentary studio photography.

### Choose neutral backgrounds
The point of most documentary studio photography is to emphasize the object. Therefore leave out velvets, props, rocks, old boots, burlap, scenery and so on. Some professionals overdo an image, insisting it be a great 'photograph.' We, however, want to concentrate on the object and so in general stick to white or neutral gray backgrounds. Colored backgrounds can lead to poor images and I recommend that you stay simple for a bit before experimenting with colors, textures, scenery or reflective shooting surfaces next to your work.

### The drop shadow box
At this point I'd like to discuss how we can go about building a drop shadow box. The point of having one is to be able to control the light falling onto the object by a combination of a moveable roof and flaps and to have the upper rear of the shooting surface actually in shadow rather than relying on light metering to produce the drop shadow effect.

For a start, it's good to do this in a basement (this is where I have mine), simply because you have rafters (actually floor joists) in a basement, and you can clamp lights to them above the shooting area and hang things off them and this makes life a lot easier. However, let's say you didn't have a basement beam above available to clamp lights onto. Then you have to build a central beam above the shooting area, which projects forwards from over the shooting surface and drop shadow box. This overhead beam is supported by a vertical one at the rear of the drop shadow box.

To reiterate: the main parts of a drop shadow box are a vertical beam at the rear of the box and a horizontal beam projecting forwards from the top of the vertical beam (onto which lights get clamped). There is a table or surface on which the object is placed. Above this shooting surface there is a flat square of stiff material which can move up and down and tilt back and forth: a roof. From three sides of this roof hang opaque cloth-like flaps. At the sides of the booth are two photofloods on light stands. Above is a third, stronger light source. All these things control the light falling onto the object from the front and the sides.

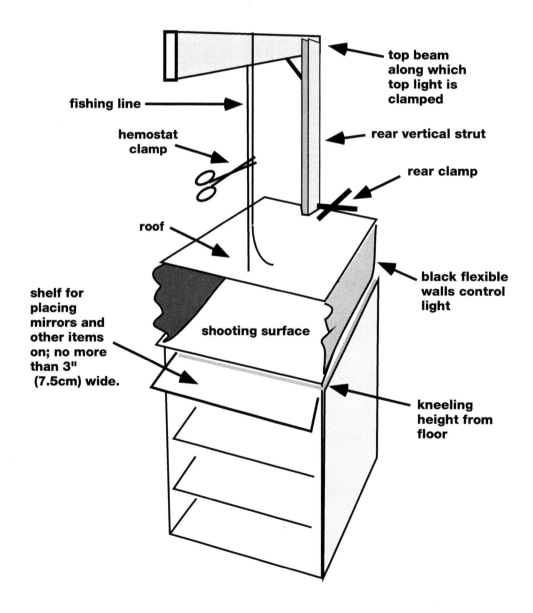

Figure 9

## How to make the drop shadow box

We begin by taking a strut of wood for the back vertical beam, say a beam that is an inch to an inch and a half square, and we attach it, if possible, to a wall. This is at the rear of the shooting surface. We will be using this vertical beam to clamp the rear of the roof to at different heights.

If we're not in a basement, we will also have at the very top of the vertical beam another beam, a plank of wood that extends outward over the shooting surface high enough not to get in our way as we work, and this allows us to clamp lights onto it above the shooting surface and at varying distances from the object by moving the clamp-on lights back and forth along the beam. To make the roof we take a piece of stiff material - I like Coroplast®, which is the material that real estate people use for their signs, but you can use Foam-Core® or stiff cardboard or something like that as well. I would make mine about three feet square. This is designed so that if you create two slits into the Coroplast® at the back so as to fit onto the vertical beam, you get a small flap, and the Coroplast® can now be clamped onto the vertical beam with one of those spring clamps that you get in hardware stores that have orange plastic on the handle. The square roof sheet can now move up and down the beam very smoothly, can be fixed in place, and because it's on a flap at the back it works like a hinge and the front end can pivot up and down as well. We can now take some fishing line or string and attach it to the front of our square roof, run this fishing line or string over the horizontal beam above and back down again. The string is clamped with a hemostat (a hemostat is what they use in operations to quickly clamp blood vessels with. When they use them they're only good for one use, so if you know anyone who works in a hospital or in an operating room, they can usually get you hemostats fairly easily). Shops like Radio Shack also stock them. The advantage of using the hemostat is that it's a quick clamping device, so that in an instant, I can pull on the cord, raise the front of the roof sheet up or let it down to allow more or less light in, and reclamp the cord rapidly in order to keep the roof sheet in place. We now have a roof, which can move easily up and down, which can pivot up and down from the back allowing the front or the back to tilt. This allows light to fall in and past the roof onto the shooting surface beneath it. I like to have the inside of the roof white as a reflector above the object on the shooting surface.

We now take black plastic garbage bags or black cloth and cut them with scissors to create three flaps that hang off the back and the two sides of the roof sheet. These are probably attached with duct tape or gaffer tape - the photographer's friend (duct tape is a poor imitation of the photo professional's gaffer tape). Each flap is independent and separate from the others: there's one hanging from the back, and there's one on each side of the roof sheet. Because they're a flexible fabric-like material, they can be lifted up, tucked over out of the way to let light in from the sides, or they can hang down. Most of the time all three of them hang down in place. What we are beginning to construct is ways of letting light in or keeping it out from under the roof sheet. Our construction now: the whole roof can move up and down to let more or less light in, the roof can be tilted up or down at the front easily for the same reason and the sides can be lifted up or down, again to control the light.

Now, we need some sort of a base that we're going to be placing objects on. You can use a small table (one can sometimes use a cardboard box) and this sits underneath the roof. This 'table' is similar in size to the roof but comes out a little in front of it.

I suggest a shelf just below the level of the shooting surface at the front. This shelf is a place, among other things, for mirrors to be positioned. The shelf should not be wider than about 3" (7.5 cm) because then it can interfere with camera positioning for very close-up shots of pieces on the shooting surface.

**Kneeling height**

The height of the shooting surface is interesting, because I like to make it at kneeling height, that is, when I am kneeling the camera viewfinder is at a comfortable height for me to look through at the object on the shooting surface. I put a foam hiking pad on the floor, and when I kneel on it that gives me a good height to work at. The reason for this is that there are times when you wish to have a very high vertical view of an object, and if your drop shadow system is any higher than kneeling height you can't extend the tripod high enough to get the shot you need, whereas if you start at kneeling height, you have a lot more leeway in your angles and how far off the surface you can come to take pictures, thus the fairly low height from the floor. Because your kneeling height will be different than mine I won't give an exact measurement for this.

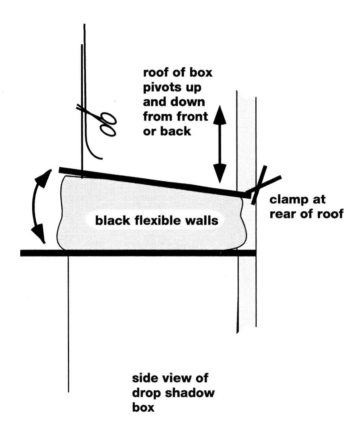

Figure 9.1

I might suggest extenders of some kind at each side of the shooting surface. These extenders come out diagonally on each side of you as you take the photograph. Ones like these are part of my own photo-booth and are inclined upwards slightly so that the mirrors can sit on them in ranked heights so as to better modulate the light that is happening inside the box.

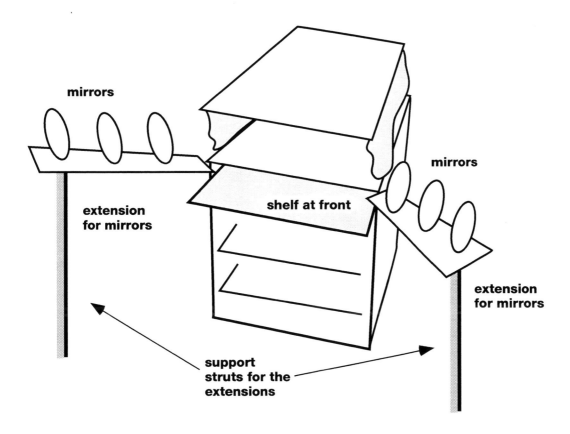

Figure 9.2

## The shooting surface

At this point, we now need a shooting surface. I like to use charcoal gray paper which can be purchased at most art supply stores. This is relatively inexpensive and it's a nice neutral tone. This is attached at the far interior side of the roof with duct tape, and it falls down towards the front in a smooth, even swoop. I often take black spray paint, and I will spray paint the far end of that charcoal gray paper from a distance so the paint lands in light speckles and it physically, actually gets darker towards the top inside the box. One can buy seamless paper at a photo shop fairly inexpensively in various widths and all kinds of colors. I suggest sticking with gray until you have some experience. It is simplest, easiest and works well. Our object will sit near the front of it on the shooting surface formed by the paper.

## Other types of shooting surfaces

Once you have some experience you may wish to consider other materials for your backdrop. Many photographers use plain white paper, and they modulate what you see by observing very carefully what's happening with the light, metering and setting the exposure for a strong lighting level on the object and thus controlling it, so that you might at the first glance at a slide of an object on white think you were actually seeing it on a light gray surface.

We can get Color-Aid® paper which is an extremely expensive clay-coated paper that comes in five hundred different colors and full tonal bleeds across a sheet - from dark to light in a single shade of color. They are clay-coated - that is if you breathe on them wrongly they scratch and you've just lost thirty dollars - but they're really nice papers for a shooting surface.

Some professionals will use linoleum, because linoleum can easily be repainted rapidly to produce different colors. Again, for our compromise box, we don't want to have to do any work; we just want to walk in and put items in and take a picture. Again, I like charcoal gray paper, and that's what I recommend. You can experiment with different shooting surfaces: tile, plastic surfaces of different kinds such as black Plexiglas (Perspex). This can be particularly good because of its black reflections. Formica-type kitchen counter materials can also be used.

When I started out I took photographs on black velvet (ooh - dust shows up) inside a light tent on a vertical copy stand which does make the colors of the object stand out in a very dramatic, lovely manner. However some photographers and magazine editors hate shots on black velvet because they feel the object is floating in space and has no connection to the earth. Basically I think it is now seen as a little old-fashioned and the drop shadow effect we are trying for in this book has superseded black velvet as a 'standard' shot type for reproduction. Because it is now a rare type of background this means that there is a place for black velvet and you might want to try it sometime and see what you think. Meltzer really likes it and uses black flocked background paper from photo stores. He does not recommend it for dark/colored objects, but instead for lighter objects and bright colors. To get the proper light reading lean the camera forwards to take the reading with the object filling the viewfinder or use a gray card (Meltzer, p 54-55).

Sometimes I will have to photograph a person's torso and head wearing a necklace or a hat. I will buy old movie projection screens at the flea market, spray paint them with a light gray speckle and use them as a background surface for this. They cost about $5.00 and if they break the tripod portion can still serve as a light stand.

## How the Lights are Rigged

We should discuss how the lights are rigged. I explained that we had a vertical beam or strut that rose up from the back of the photo-booth and from which a horizontal beam came out above our entire drop shadow box, that we had a shooting surface on which we were taking a picture, above that we had our rigid flap which moves up and down as a whole or just at the front or back, and our three black plastic or cloth sides. Above everything and slightly in front of the photo-booth we have a large clamp-on light with a 500 watt photoflood bulb. You want the top light to have a fairly large bell - the bigger the better. This can be clamped onto the vertical beam and moved in and out, away from or towards the shooting surface, so the light can be angled to enter more or less into the box to suit one's need. It normally has a large sheet of Mylar® clothespinned to it as a diffusion screen. It is often positioned above and somewhat behind the camera position. The bulb is about four feet from the object itself.

On each side of the drop shadow box we have a 250 watt photoflood bulb, somewhat above the roof height and angled downwards towards it. These two are somewhat in front of the photo-booth. The bulbs themselves are about three feet from the object itself. These need to be on some kind of vertical upright stand or tripod. At its simplest, that could be a construction of plywood: a square of plywood with a vertical plank attached to it, and you could move the clamp-on light up and down and the whole wooden stand in and out to control the lighting position. What I tend to do is to shop at flea markets and purchase music stands or other inexpensive tripods, and use those for my clamp-on lights at the sides of the photo-booth.

**View from side of drop shadow booth and how the light falls towards the opening in the box. Diffusers have been left off for clarity.**

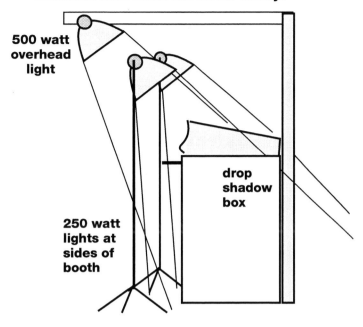

**500 watt overhead light**

**drop shadow box**

**250 watt lights at sides of booth**

Figure 10

**View from top of drop shadow booth of how the light falls towards the opening in the box**

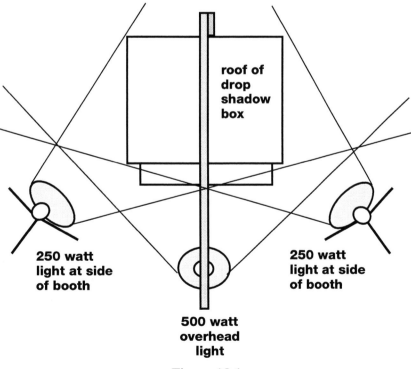

**roof of drop shadow box**

**250 watt light at side of booth**

**250 watt light at side of booth**

**500 watt overhead light**

Figure 10.1

On the sides, then, we have two clamp-on lights that can be moved up and down and in and out. These clamp-on lights on the side are at about 45 to 60 degrees to the shooting surface and help us to modulate how much light falls into the box. They are positioned fairly high so their light falls downwards onto the object and the opening of the photo-booth. So you can see that the system gives us a very great deal of control over how the light falls in, what it does, and how it's used. Each of these clamp-on lights has a diffuser attached to it; I recommend translucent Mylar®. You can use tracing paper, but architectural Mylar® is the best in my experience. Wooden clothespins are very effective as clamps for this, are cheap and rapid to use. With our system we want to be able to move things around quickly and make decisions rapidly.

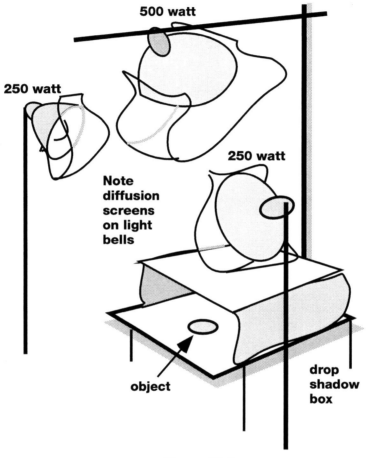

Figure 10.2

On the clamp-on light bells at the sides, the Mylar® hangs from the top edge and down, held in place by clothespins. This diffuses the light, and gives us the kind of light that photographers prefer. A photographer's dream light might be ten o'clock in the winter in a studio that's a big, giant, white room, with all windows on one side, facing north, on a semi-cloudy day. Nice diffuse light that's bouncing off a lot of white surfaces, and that's what we're after here, our light falling through the diffusers towards our shooting surface and our object. On the top light, the one with the 500 watt bulb, we have a very large sheet of Mylar® clothespinned onto both sides of the spun aluminum bell: the bigger the better.

**Diffusion options**
Diffuse light is in general the best lighting for most shots. A large surface area of diffuse, gentle light from above is a very important part of much professional photography (ceramics and glass in particular seem to do well with this). A photographer would call the specialized light unit for

34

this a 'soft box.' In our system the top light with its large Mylar® diffusion sheet held in place with clothespins is our 'soft box.' Some people construct an enclosed Foam-Core® and Mylar® version of a professional soft box but our version allows soft diffused light to fall on the object from above as well as spilling hard light out the sides that is then used both to raise the ambient light around the photo set-up and is reflected from mirrors to further model the light falling on the object. Diffuse light is called soft light and direct light from the bulb or light source is called hard light.

When using diffusion screens anywhere near hot bulbs you have to be aware of the danger of heat and potential fire, so any diffusion screen must not come too close to a bulb. It should stay at least four to five inches (10-15 cm) away from the source of heat, otherwise you could start a fire. Always have one and preferably two ABC fire extinguishers just next to the photo area and make sure they are maintained properly and checked annually by your fire department. Make sure a licensed electrician has checked over your wiring and lighting system to avoid the potential for an electrical fire.

Burning oneself on hot bulbs, edges of metal light bells and so on is also a hazard. If you do get burned it is most important to freeze or cool a burn as quickly as possible and keep it frozen or cold for a long time to prevent further burning. I've stopped (or at least ameliorated) burns by rapidly packing snow or ice cubes onto them. A former student chilled a burn with repeated rounds of cold soda cans from a vending machine.

The purpose of the diffusion screens in front of the light bulbs is to blend the light - to make the light softer and to cut down on contrast. When you're taking color photographs, it's difficult to see contrast accurately: in fact when you're taking any photograph, it is difficult to see and understand the contrast you are looking at until you have some practice at it, so it's easy to shoot things that are too contrasty. If we have everything lit softly we will generally tend to get better results. What we're doing is obtaining a diffuse light, either by having the light softened by bouncing off white surfaces before it hits our object, or by filtering the light through diffusion screens before it hits it.

It helps if you can paint the area around the photo-booth white (especially useful in a basement). The more light around the system the better and if you have white surfaces in the vicinity this helps.

Using two clothespins for clamping diffusion screens onto the reflector bell of the clamp-on light allows you to alter lighting positions very quickly. I usually slit the Mylar® near the edge of the sheet to allow the clothespin to pass through it to clamp it onto the edge of the aluminum reflector bell.

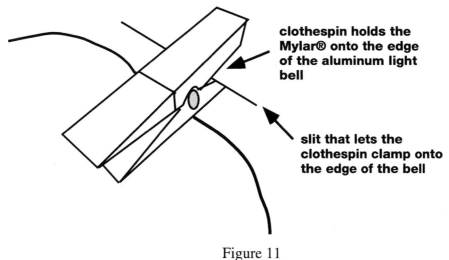

**clothespin holds the Mylar® onto the edge of the aluminum light bell**

**slit that lets the clothespin clamp onto the edge of the bell**

Figure 11

This is the position in which I use the diffuser on the overhead 500 watt light bell: with both sides of the large sheet of Mylar® clothespinned onto each side of the light bell.

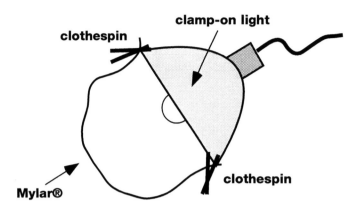

Figure 11.1

If you release the clothespin on the side away from the object then the Mylar® hangs down in front, diffuse light spills forwards onto the object and hard light spills out sideways and downwards, allowing us to catch it on mirrors to produce small spotlights to modulate the light effects on the object. This is the most common position in which I use the diffusion screens on the lights at the sides of the booth.

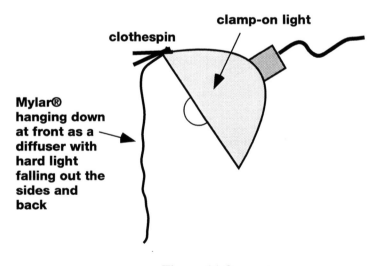

Figure 11.2

If, instead, the clothespin closest to the object is released then the hard light spills onto the object directly from the bulb and the Mylar® hangs down behind acting as a reflector, thus adding to the amount of light falling onto the object. One rarely uses this last position, however, as hard light often results in poor photographs.

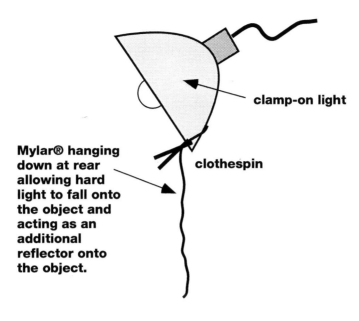

**Mylar® hanging down at rear allowing hard light to fall onto the object and acting as an additional reflector onto the object.**

**clamp-on light**

**clothespin**

Figure 11.3

Professional photographers may have a slightly different approach here, and I'll just mention it: instead of having the diffusion screens close to the light, and the lights some distance from the object as I suggest, they often place the diffusion screens very close to the object and bring the lights in close as well. This increases the local light levels which can have some advantages in very long exposures - longer exposures than will be the case most of the time in our drop shadow system.

### How the mirrors are rigged

There's a fair bit of hard light, that is, non-diffuse light, which is falling out the sides of our clamp-on lighting system. We catch this hard light on mirrors and reflect it towards the object being photographed as spotlighting and fill lighting (light that brightens deeply shadowed areas on the object). Therefore we have mirrors all around, on the shooting surface itself, and perhaps on extensions that we build out from the sides of the photo-booth shooting area. The mirrors allow one to use front lighting and side lighting to model the object.

### Hot spots

With even slightly reflective objects you have to make sure that you don't have a 'hot spot,' a place that is really bright and thus overpowers the image or messes up your ability to resolve detail on the film. A hot spot can be a glaring patch or simply a small spot that is too bright by comparison with the rest of the image. It is a place where you've got too much light, and it can alter your light reading if you are not aware of what you are doing, so you have to watch out for having too much light in a certain place.

Make sure that, if you have a really bright hot spot, you modulate it down. With swinging mirrors, because they change position, we can modulate the degree of that hot spot quite easily.

Hot spots can be useful, just evaluate how and what purpose they serve: often they can help describe a surface but need moderating to the most useful point. The mirrors give us enormous control over this aspect of lighting.

So, watch out for hot spots. Hot spots are easy to miss, particularly when starting out. In general, if a place on the object is really bright, watch it, check it: tone it down.

**Fill cards**

Fill cards are white cards, pieces of paper, Styrofoam or Foam-Core® which are used as light reflectors to 'fill' in deeply shadowed areas of an object: to lighten them. We are in general trying for an overall average feel to the lighting of an object and fill cards allow us to light areas that are either in shadow or are too dark by comparison with the rest of the object.

We have to take into account how the light meter, the camera and the film 'see' the object. If you have too large a range of lighting conditions and you meter for what is too dark on the object then all the light areas fade out into overexposed lightness; if you meter for what is too light then all the dark areas just turn black and you can't see any detail in them. Fill cards allow you to bounce light back across a surface towards the light source it is coming from and thus even out the lighting on the object so you can record as much detail as possible about the entire object.

Fill cards are usually placed fairly close to the object. An example that Collins uses is lighting a quilt with a single light source from the upper left-hand side (a 'raking angle') in order to bring out the texture and then using a large fill card at the right-hand edge to return some of the light back across the surface (Collins, 96). I use fill cards a lot but find that judicious use of the mirrors takes the place of a fair bit of fill card work. There is usually a combination of fill cards and mirrors near the objects I am shooting.

**Back lighting**

Sometimes an object can be made to stand out well against the inside of the drop shadow box by lighting the shooting surface behind it where it curves up inside the box. This provides a 'halo' of lighter background behind the object, or just a part of the object, and there are times when this is a very effective way of shooting an object. We can create such a back lighting effect using our mirrors selectively to lighten the shooting surface far inside the rear of the box. A caution: in your final checking before you take a photograph you should always check for stray light spots inside your booth; having mirrors around can sometimes give you such an effect where you don't want it. Another way of approaching lighting the background behind the object is discussed a little later in the section 'Shooting on glass in a frame.'

**Aluminum foil**

Aluminum foil can serve as a reflector at times. I sometimes glue it to a sheet of Foam-Core® as a flat reflector. It produces 'specular' highlights - sort of water-like reflections - and has to be used with caution. As highly reflective 'fill cards' they can be smooth or wrinkly; in general smooth is better and some people put a diffuser over them to lower the hardness of light reflected from them. I have used the aluminum-foil-coated inside surfaces of the round Chinese food container tops that one sometimes gets for take-out food as reflectors. They are easy to cut and bend into small, self-supporting reflective stands because the foil is smoothly bonded to the cardboard top. I do use aluminum foil to light the insides of things like cups or goblets. I crumple it up inside the cup, usually near the front inside surface of the vessel. Then it gathers light (particularly if I can feed some light into the cup with a mirror, a fill card or a fiber optic light) and lights the far inside of the cup that is visible to the camera thus lending a small drama and life to the cup.

**Colored papers**

Colored paper strips and pieces can be used to add color to an object by reflecting in it but it is rather unusual to use them; there is just too much chance of producing a bad image with them. Same thing goes for colored gels over the lights or mirrors.

Sometimes, however, one does use colored paper to modulate the light, and how it looks on the object. So, for instance, reflective silver often looks extremely white in a lighting tent (see

'Reflective Objects'), so sometimes people will place a small strip of blue paper nearby. Blue is associated with silver, and that little hint of bluish tone to the surface often makes the reader, the viewer, understand the object as silver. In gold, sometimes if one has a polished gold ring or something, and it's reflecting the sides of the box and so on then one places a small piece of yellow paper close by, to lend the object the gold color that the viewer expects. But normally one isn't doing these kinds of things too much; just very occasionally.

### Paper backings
Sometimes I have run across the problem of having a transparent quartz crystal jutting off an object or a glass piece which shows the blackness of the drop shadow booth behind through it and so virtually 'disappears' from the shot. In this case a carefully cut piece of translucent or white paper cut out and shaped to cover the rear of the object or transparent part helps. This allows one to see the transparent part against the drop shadow background. One must however in any such manipulation check and test to see if one is changing the perception of the object. The point is to emphasize and show what is there, not to create a piece that doesn't exist in real life.

## Holding Objects for Photography

If an object will sit by itself on the shooting surface this is not a problem but often it needs to be propped up in some way. Even objects that will sit well on a flat surface sometimes need tilting slightly towards the camera by placing something under their rear side. Holding an object in place for the photograph is usually fairly easy and fast just by placing a suitable chunk of something heavy behind it against which it can lean. Wedges of wood or other materials can be useful for this. In general keep your holding method as simple, straightforward, rapid and clean as possible.

### Steel blocks
I use small steel blocks cut from square rod that I can stack on top of each other until I get a stack high enough and heavy enough to keep the object in place by propping it against the stack. The blocks are about 1/2" (1.5 cm) thick and vary in length though most are about 2" (5 cm) long. One can also use large steel nuts from bolts, heavy washers and so on as long as they are clean and don't stain the shooting surface (spray paint cans can serve for medium-sized objects). Square and rectangular pieces of scrap steel are useful. I often put a small blob of Fun-Tack® onto the front of the top steel block to ensure the object doesn't move. I have more than one intriguing slide of an object blurring as it falls or swivels just at the moment the picture was taken. You also don't want to see anything that is propping up your object from the front view, and therefore looking for something peeking out from behind it is an important final check before taking a photograph.

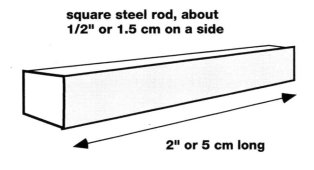

Figure 12

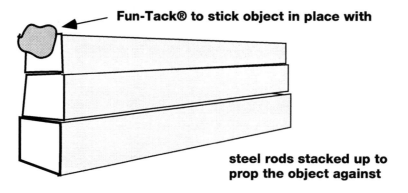

**Fun-Tack® to stick object in place with**

**steel rods stacked up to prop the object against**

Figure 12.1

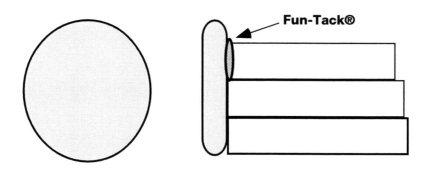

**Fun-Tack®**

Figure 12.2

## Fun-Tack®

I use Fun-Tack® to help hold objects up. This is a material that you can buy at the stationary store for putting up posters that is not supposed to (but does) damage a painted wall. With a small blob of it against your support even a tippy object is helped to stay put. I often use Fun-Tack® just to stick an object onto a chunk of steel, or to stick the object itself onto the shooting surface. Fun-Tack® will not damage your shooting surface. You don't want to use beeswax or Plasticine to hold an object up, because these will stain the shooting surface, and may also affect the object. Plasticine, for instance, contains sulfur, which will darken and blacken most metals within a pretty short period of time. A warning about the Fun-Tack®: it turns silver black if it's in contact with it for some time, so you have to be careful when using it with jewelry. It is fine in contact with metals for an hour or so-just don't leave it overnight. Hot glue is another method for holding objects up but I don't often use it as it takes time to warm the glue gun, damages the paper if it touches it, works well on metals and smooth objects but can damage others. There is the occasional time, however, when hot glue might be a useful solution to a propping problem.

## Stainless wire

As well as steel blocks, we can use stainless steel wire stands to hold our objects up. We can make a small hole in our nice charcoal gray shooting surface through which we can slide a thin stainless steel wire from below. The base of the wire is bent around with pliers to form a flat spiral which sits under the shooting surface. The paper presses onto the spiral beneath it and keeps the upright wire section stiff and steady. An object (even a thin or awkward one) can be propped against the wire and if necessary a small blob of Fun-Tack® can hold the object in place on it. We could use piano wire instead, which you can buy at most hobby stores, but the piano wire rusts and will tend to stain the shooting surface, so I prefer the stainless steel wire. It can be obtained from orthodontists but the least expensive source I have found is Small Parts Inc. (see sources). I use this quite a bit, and one thing that I might recommend would be to place that hole slightly off to one side in your shooting surface, so that you don't disturb the central area of the shooting surface with a hole. The hole is not very obtrusive, but still, it's there. Make it as small as possible.

It's also possible to curve the stainless steel wire above the shooting surface for specific propping problems - for instance, I once shot a flexible bracelet which was stuck onto a curved wire and this bracelet appeared to be rising from the surface and flying through the air in the photograph because it was attached to the wire.

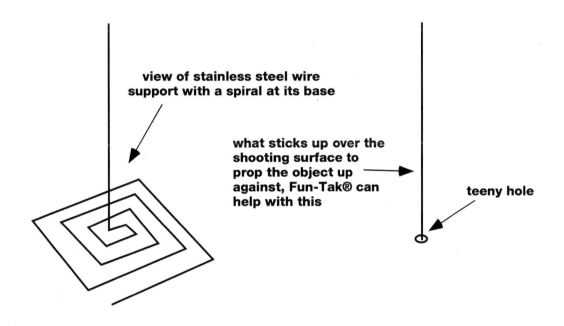

Figure 12.3

**Fishing line**
Fishing line can sometimes be quite useful. We might use fishing line for suspending earrings or a pendant or something like that. It might be clamped in place with clothespins on each side of the roof of the drop shadow box allowing us to hang the object so it 'floats.' The trouble is that the fishing line tends to show up in the photograph, because it catches the light. If you run a little black magic marker across the fishing line, you can often kill it completely and make it disappear. Fishing line is, however, a little tricky, so I would normally recommend using the stainless steel wire supports or a prop of some kind if at all possible. Black nylon thread could be used instead of fishing line. Certain objects are best photographed using a glass-topped frame as is described near the end of this section.

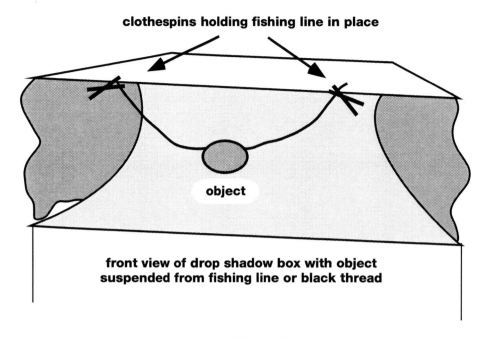

Figure 12.4

## Rear supporting rod

Another thing that works quite well is a rear supporting rod. Have different lengths of rod available for different problems. Examples of rod materials include dowel, steel welding rod, brass brazing rod, knitting needles and so on. Useful rod lengths might be 8" (18 cm), 12" (30 cm), 15" (38 cm). This one shown has been made from a jeweler's third arm, which is a clamping device that pivots, and there's a rod been installed in it, so that it projects outwards and can be positioned at different angles. If you put a blob of Fun-Tack® on the end of it, you can place an object of jewelry or another small object here, and have the rod projecting from the back of the box forward, so that the object is quite literally floating in the air in our drop shadow situation. If you are careful, you may be able to set things up so that your object completely covers up the stand, and you don't see it at all. If, however, some of the stand is still visible behind the object, then we work with depth of field to eliminate it from the photograph; to make the stand so out of focus no one can see it. I usually spray paint such stands with a matte flat black. A third arm stand like this can be purchased at electronics shops such as Radio Shack or at a jewelers' supply store.

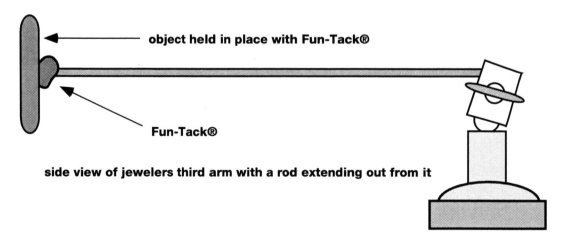

Figure 12.5

Another way to obtain a similar effect is to stick a rod through the shooting surface from behind and stick the object onto the front of it with Fun - Tack® or hot glue. I don't often use this method however as I hate damaging my shooting surface in the drop shadow box. If you damage it you may need to change it and the whole idea is to have to change as little as possible while you are shooting. Changing things takes time.

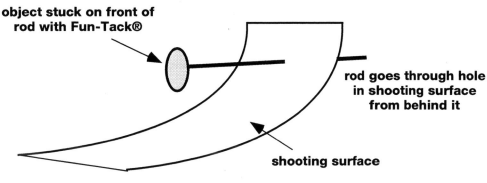

Figure 12.6

Again, we can set things up with our camera using depth of field so that only a very short band or thickness of the object is in focus and if we do that carefully, we can make it so that the stand behind completely disappears, just goes completely out of focus and the only thing in focus is our object that's floating in the air. We would set the f-stop on the lens to f-8 or so to do this (see the section "Depth of Field").

**Shooting on glass in a frame**
Objects like pendants, earrings and other hard-to-prop-up-or-support items can be shot on a glass-topped shooting surface: on a piece of glare-free glass. Glare-free glass can be obtained from photo suppliers but one can use ordinary glass if one is careful. One can also use frosted glasses and plastic translucent materials of various kinds.

One takes a piece of very clear, very clean glass and sets it up on top of a frame of some kind. A quick one can be done with the glass supported on each side by a chair or box. A permanent one is constructed from wood. One places the backdrop paper underneath the glass. One can experiment with all kinds of interesting lighting effects behind the object on the backdrop paper (back lighting) such as giving the object a 'halo' by shining the lights in underneath the object from the sides. The object is placed in the center of the glass and you take the picture with the camera facing down at the object. The object itself is lit from above with a 'soft box' (large diffuse light source) and otherwise conventionally lit so as to stand out against the background, which may be lit as described above or be darkened to produce a drop shadow effect behind the lit object which then magically floats over the drop shadow background. This approach gives extremely good results, and you don't see the glass at all if you angle the camera and lights correctly. There's often a little bit of messing around to make sure that there's no reflection or glare off the glass to the camera (possibly a time for a polarizing filter). Dust and things that land on the glass can be an irritant in this approach. It can however give you very lovely results and it's a pretty easy set-up.

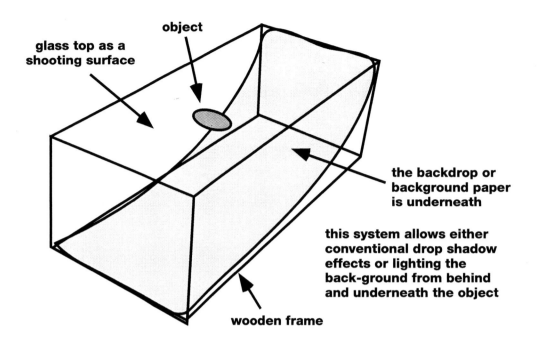

**object**

**glass top as a shooting surface**

**the backdrop or background paper is underneath**

**this system allows either conventional drop shadow effects or lighting the back-ground from behind and underneath the object**

**wooden frame**

Figure 12.7

# Depth of Field

Depth of field refers to the amount of the object that is in focus (the depth that is in focus). When you look through the camera's viewfinder on a close-up shot you may notice that part of the object is in focus and part is not. You can change the focus using the lens so that the front, middle or back zone of the object is in focus. You will, however, not normally be able to see the entire object in focus at the same time throughout the viewfinder. However, what you see in focus and what the camera (and film) see in focus is not the same thing. Luckily we can arrange matters so that, even if we can't see everything in focus at the same time through the viewfinder, the camera and film can. In a final image the amount of the object that is in focus is very important. In general we want all of the object in focus.

On your camera lens, you have f-stops. What the f-stops do is open and close an iris diaphragm inside the lens that allows more or less light inside the camera (this is called varying the aperture). If we have the camera lens set on f-2.8 or f-4 or so, we're letting a lot of light into the camera: the hole that lets the light in is open wide. If we have it set on f-16, f-22, f-32, then we're letting a lot less light into the camera: the iris diaphragm is closed up very small. In order to take the picture if we have the lens set on f-22 or f-16 (so there's not much light coming in), we have to take a longer exposure to get the same image (keep the shutter open a longer time). If we had it set on f-8, letting a lot of light in, then we would be able to use a much shorter exposure time for the same image. The less light you let in, the more of the object is in focus.

The less light you let in (the smaller the aperture), and the longer exposure you need, the more depth of field you will have and the more of your object will be in focus for the camera and the film. On the other hand the more light you let into the camera, the less depth of field you have, the less of your object will be in focus. Again, most of the time with three-dimensional objects we are concerned with having all of them in focus, so that most of the time with this system we will be shooting if possible with the f-stop at f-22 or at f-16. There is little point to going beyond that; even if your camera goes to f-32, as I understand it, f-22 would be the best choice for you.

The smaller an object, and the closer you are to it, the less depth of field you have available, so that, for instance, in microscopy, where they're taking pictures of bacteria and really tiny objects on a glass slide, their depth of field is almost non-existent; it's a single plane. In our case here, where we're pretty close to an object, depth of field becomes an issue. Again, most of the time we will solve this by setting the f-stop at f-22 and adjusting the shutter speed until we get the correct light meter reading to allow us to take the picture. Most often, that shutter speed will be one second or so, but of course you'll have to check for the right combination of f-stop and exposure time yourself when you are taking a specific photograph.

Commercial photographers will go to extremes to obtain greater depth of field; they may have an exposure of a minute, or sometimes a number of minutes long in order to have a large object or a tabletop composition all in focus. This kind of long exposure requires very good equipment, absolutely no vibration, high light levels and lots more experience and theoretical knowledge than can be dealt with in this book. With a 35 mm SLR camera you are generally dealing with a one second or so exposure for the system we are using. Dan Gordon points out that tungsten films will handle exposures of 30 seconds or more without problems.

I described earlier how we could deliberately use depth of field to arrange things so that our rear support stand is out of focus and our object is in focus, and here's an example: let's say that I had a rather flat object, and it was on a rod projecting from a stand at the back of the drop shadow shooting surface and I could see some of the stand behind the object. I might set the camera on f-8 or f-4, and reduce my depth of field so that only the flat plane of the object was in focus, making the visible parts of the stand go strongly out of focus and thus blend in with the background. We would now use the depth of field preview button to see what the camera is actually seeing.

If we increase the local light levels, then this allows us to use a faster shutter speed with a small f-stop (small f-stop equals better depth of field), and that offers a little more flexibility. This is one of the reasons why professionals often bring the lights in close. The closer you bring the lights, the more light, and hence the more control you have (more or less) of the depth of field; the more light you have, the better depth of field you can have at a given shutter speed. This does however have drawbacks. A photographer friend of mine who does a lot of food photography told me one time about shooting a bowl of strawberries and ice cream. Basically they had a four-sided translucent white box around it and were shooting straight down at the bowl. The lights were all about a foot away from the bowl of ice cream and fresh strawberries. They went through 50 bowls of ice cream, because every time they put one in to take a shot, the heat from the lights would melt the ice cream almost immediately, so it was like, "Quick, quick, move now, shoot and do it again - let's have another bowl."

Again, for our drop shadow box I suggest sticking to the formula given for awhile and having the lights at some distance from the object; that's what allows us to use our mirrors and it is the mirrors that make the system excellent. After awhile, experiment with bringing the lights in closer and see what you think of the approach.

### How to use the depth of field preview button
The depth of field preview button is usually on the front right of the camera. You push it in order to see what the camera and film are really going to see, and to find out what's in focus and not. Again, what you see through the viewfinder is not what the camera and film see.

So, if I am looking at an object, and I've focused on it, and I've set the camera lens at f-22 perhaps, and perhaps it's at a one second shutter speed, depending upon what my lighting is like, I will still see most of my object out of focus through the viewfinder. To see what the camera is seeing, I press the depth of field preview button. Everything immediately gets darker because I'm now seeing what the camera's seeing through this little tiny hole - f-22, not much light coming in; however, with the depth of field preview button pressed, I will see whatever is in focus, even though it's dark.

Begin by focusing about one third of the way back into the object. Because what you can see darkens quite considerably when you press the button (and it is hard to see if the object is in focus or not), the way you deal with it is to look through the viewfinder and establish some bright spots on your object, some light streaks, or glints of light at the front of the object that are out of focus, and at the rear of the object that are out of focus. Look at the edges where you placed your side lighting to define and frame the object against the background to find such bright glints of light. Now press the depth of field preview button, and if those sharp light spots come into focus, you know your whole object is in focus. So the depth of field preview button allows you to see what the camera sees, and that's really, really useful.

### Standard focus position (1/3 in)
A general rule of thumb that works most of the time is to use f-16 or f-22 and to focus through the viewfinder to one third of the way back into the object. That means that when you look through the viewfinder, a point one third of the way back into the object is in focus. You can check to see how much is really in focus using the depth of field preview button but most of the time this 'one third back' rule works out well.

### What you see is not what you get
When you look through the lens, as I said, you don't necessarily see what the camera sees; another thing you don't necessarily see is how much image area you're actually going to get on the film. Some cameras give you more surface area than you see through the viewfinder, and some cameras give you a little bit less surface area than you can see. If you're using a camera that you're not familiar with, I recommend taking a sheet of gridded paper, writing numbers on it, and taking a picture of that grid. When you get it back from the photo processor, and after it's slide mounted, have a look and see how much you've gained or how much you've lost, because you need to know exactly what you're going to get on the slides. The Nikon F2 and F3 are apparently the only cameras around which actually show you same amount of image through the viewfinder that will appear on the film. You should also take into account that if you're shooting slides, after the transparency goes inside the slide mount, you lose some of the area around the edges of the shot; the slide mount will crop your image a bit. This is why you don't have an object too large in the shot, too close to the edges of the frame.

# Preparing the Camera

### Loading the camera
Load and unload the camera in subdued light. When installing a roll of film, pull the leader out of the cassette for several inches. Install the leader into the take-up spool first, wind it on to make sure it really is winding around the spool. Once you see that it's winding on and around the take-up spool and that it's not going to slip out, then pull the cassette across to the left, plant the film into the left side of the camera, close the back and lock it in place. The reason for this is that it's really frustrating if you go and shoot 36 shots and then find that the film never wound on and you have to do it all over again. Always make sure that the film is actually winding on before you close the back of the camera. This action will prevent you from having a film which did not wind on-voice of experience.

Kink the end of the leader sharply against itself before inserting it into the take-up spool. This helps you wind it on better and is useful if there are times when you need to change films partway through a shoot. You might for instance be using some black and white film and want to change to a color film type without shooting up the roll you have in the camera. So then, after noting the number of frames you have already shot on the roll, you rewind the film in the camera very slowly and carefully. When the bent-over kink at the end leaves the take-up spool it will make an audible click, and that's why we bent it back - so you can hear it and avoid winding the film all the way back into the cassette; once you do that it's a real pain in the neck to try and get the little leader out again. Then you take the film out, put it aside, and on the film can you write "shot 10, such and such a date." When you want to use that film again, you put it back in the camera, with the lens cover cap on so you don't double-expose the previously shot film, and shoot probably to 12 on the film counter - wind, click, wind, click, wind, click and when you hit 12, you're now in unexposed film again, and you can take the lens cover off and just go on and use the rest of the roll. If you do wind a film all the way in by accident camera shops sell a film leader removal tool but will probably fish the film leader out for you if you ask.

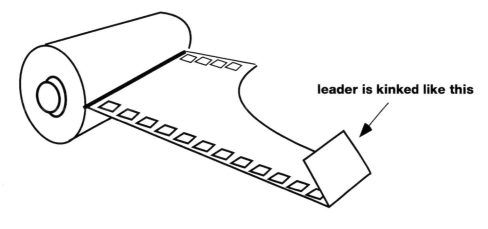

leader is kinked like this

Figure 13

### Check your battery and ISO every time
This too is the voice of experience. I strongly recommend that you check your battery every time you use the camera, because it's very frustrating if you don't do that and you blow one or more rolls of film because you didn't check the battery. Also check the ISO when you use the camera in case it was shifted by accident or is inappropriate for the film type you are using. There is a small slot on the back of most cameras intended for you to slide in the flap from the box of film you are using as a reminder of what is currently in the camera. It is a good idea to use it.

# Considerations in Image Creation

### Object size and proportion in image
Now we're going to start talking about taking the picture - actually getting closer to taking the image. There's a couple of things that we need to think about. One of them is the size of the object in proportion to the image area (remember any cropping action your camera will inflict on the image seen through the viewfinder and also that you will lose some of the edge area under the slide mount). It should be just right, not too big and not too small.

**Reasonable Proportions**

Figure 14

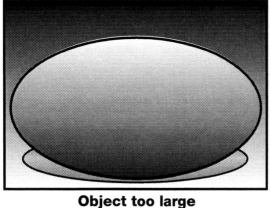

**Object too large**

Figure 14.1

**Too Small**

Figure 14.2

## Composition

Learning composition is an essential part of taking photographs. It's a bit like doing a painting, or a drawing; you have to deal with all the issues of composition that a painter, or a graphic designer, or somebody drawing something flat does. You are dealing with creating a piece of flat art (the slide or photograph), with two-dimensional composition and within the limits of the 35 mm rectangle (whose proportions as it turns out are based on the Golden Mean).

I suggest taking a 35 mm slide mount and holding it in your hand, looking at the world through it. Move it around and look at the shapes you see, experiment with relationships of line, harmony, balance and weight - that is, visual weight. Slide it around, and every now and again you'll think, "Hey, that's a good balance," or "Oh, that's a pleasant thing," or "That doesn't look good." Take it outside as well as indoors. After a while you will not need the rectangle to look through to see the compositional relationships and you will be able to get a sense of these things just by choosing to look for them. Also, when you see magazine shots, have a look at what kinds of decisions the photographer made. Remember, for documentary studio photography of objects, in general the more neutral the background the better. So composition in our terms usually has to occur within and on the object at hand and concerns how its three-dimensionality, structure and surface qualities can best be portrayed.

## Forget that it is a 3-D object

One of the hardest things about small scale photography of objects, and the one that screws you up most when you're starting, is that you must forget that the object you're looking at is a three-dimensional object, because what you're doing when you take the picture is working with a completely flat plane: the film - and the composition and the work that you're doing - has nothing to do with three dimensions. You're making a flat art object, just like working on a piece of paper.

If you get mixed up, and you imagine you are looking at a 3-D object, perhaps because you made it, and your physical experience of it as a three-dimensional object is strong, you can actually lie to yourself about what you see, and you can end up with bad pictures. So it's very important to distance yourself from the object, and when you're looking through that viewfinder, that rectangle is all there is - there's nothing else, and you're working with a flat composition. It's really important to try and remember that, because you'd be surprised how lying to yourself can make you completely miss what's happening right in front of you.

## The best view of the object
As you compose the image, search for and find the best view. But before even starting to take the picture you should decide what the image is for, what it is supposed to convey to the viewer. This means a compromise between the greatest photo, most informative, dramatic, documentary, narrative, process - revealing and other requirements of the image of the object.

Does it have a handle, an interior? What are the qualities that best fulfill the demands of the specific shot? Goals and intentions that are different will demand different considerations in the image. The best view will depend upon the function of the photograph. Usually this has to do with conveying the most textural and form information about the object - which in general means one uses a large overhead diffuse light source, small spotlighting from mirrors and side lighting to emphasize texture. One attempts to avoid overly dramatic lighting effects on the object.

## Front lighting flattens
An important basic principle about lighting your object: light directed from the front onto the object is called front lighting and front lighting flattens things, eliminates textures and relief.

Let's say you've put your object in the drop shadow box - perhaps it's an object of jewelry - you're looking through the lens and all of a sudden you see scratches that you had missed while finishing but you still need to take the picture. If you arrange your lights so they are falling directly onto the object from the front, from the direction the camera's view is from, you can almost eliminate those unwanted textures. All the scratches will disappear and you can take your shot anyway. I sometimes mount a small swiveling mirror with Fun-Tack® on top of the camera itself for this purpose.

## Side lighting picks up texture
A second important principle is that side lighting picks up texture, highlights edges and enriches relief surfaces like cloth or textured ceramic or metal. Usually in taking photographs of three-dimensional objects one is trying to emphasize and intensify the textural effects on the surface of the work. We do this by side lighting, shooting light across the surface from the sides. I usually place mirrors at each side of the object just outside of the frame and angle them to intensify the textures present.

Coins for instance might be lit primarily by side lighting to pick up the detail and subtle rounded reflective surfaces on the object.

Remember that in creating the flat art image of the photograph, one is attempting to create a 'super-real' image so the viewer can understand the object as a three-dimensional object. Because the object is reduced to a flat image by taking a photograph one has to intensify its three-dimensionality in order to convey a sense of its presence to the viewer. As well as letting us see textures and relief details, side lighting is used to create a razor-thin white edge to the sides of the object which defines its edges and makes it stand out from the background of the image. This edge lighting is very important in making a piece stand out from the background, framing it and defining it in space in the photograph.

An interesting way of subtly creating a sense of texture is to move the side lights different distances from the object; this will introduce a hint of shadow to textured areas such as cloth or cast paper. Some day if you are feeling experimental try turning different lights off one at a time in the system or moving them to different distances from the object, and observe carefully the resulting lighting effects on your object.

A traditional experiment to learn about lighting is to take a roll of photographs of a white object on a white background (an egg for instance) and make notes of different exposures, lighting methods, fill cards etc. While this is used mostly when learning about black and white photography and printing it can also be a useful exercise with color slides.

### Contrast
The issue of contrast is an interesting one (see Collins, p 115). It is difficult to see what the contrast is on an object. Try and see what is in front of you in terms of grays in order to get a sense of the contrast. You can squint and fuzz your eyes to help see this, sunglasses (perhaps those yellowish ones?) might also help. You have to reduce what you are seeing to a simple (black/white/gray) level in order to evaluate the level of contrast on the object. This will take practice and is just something to be aware of when evaluating your shot.

### Shadows
One has to be careful of shadows. Cast from the object they can either give it a sense of gravity and place on the shooting surface or look odd and distort how the viewer understands the object portrayed. Be aware of the role of shadows both on and off the object. Many professionals try and avoid them altogether by cross lighting in such a way as to eliminate them. The diffuse light we use will create soft shadows; hard shadows are caused by non-diffuse light. Although most of our light is diffuse, the mirrors we use feed non-diffuse spotlighting onto the object which can cast hard-edged shadows. I personally like to use some sense of shadow on the shooting surface in an image to 'ground' the object, but I generally like diffuse, fuzzy-edged, not-too-dark shadows.

One can do a lot on purpose using shadows. The main point is to know they are there, to look for them and to consciously choose what part they will play in the flat image you are creating on the film plane.

### Rendering and its conventions
Creating an effective image through the viewfinder leads one to use the conventions of rendering, that is, the 'normal' ways that illustrative drawing and painting are designed to transmit information. Conventions of rendering include things like: there's a strong tendency to have the strongest light source falling from the top left-hand side of the image, edges are defined by extremely thin light streaks or very thin black lines, curving tubes have a light streak that is a line on them (much like on a spool of silk thread), rounded surfaces have a curving light streak, all objects lighten near their edges even in shadowed areas, a hint of blue implies silver or chrome, a hint of brown at the base of something grounds it - and so on. So have a look at drawings and renderings to begin to think about some of the issues that you have to deal with in creating a flat image.

### Creating a super-real image
When you're creating an image like this, it is not a blind documentation of the object - you could

do that with a photocopy machine or a scanner - instead you're almost making a cartoon. You are creating a super-real image. You're taking a three-dimensional object, you're creating a piece of flat art about this object, and you want the person looking at this flat art - at the slide - to have a sense that they're seeing a three-dimensional object, so you have to take what's there and accentuate it, exaggerate it, make it more real than real. One creates an over-emphasis of what is there so that the viewer of the slide image obtains a deeper understanding of the object than would otherwise be the case. If you take a very careful look at excellent advertising photographs, you'll realize that the lighting that you're looking at is not possible in real life. Lights are coming from strange places, there are shadows that can't exist. Remember you are creating a super-real image, and it's flat.

# Taking the Photograph

The object has been chosen. The reasons for taking the photograph have been reviewed. The proportions and composition have been dealt with, the object is propped and set up on the shooting surface. It is now time to work with the lighting on the object.

### Lighting the object
Earlier we talked about how we can control the light falling into our drop shadow booth in several ways. We can lift flaps on the sides, we can lift the top up and down, we can tilt the roof up and away from or down towards the opening of the box; we can move our exterior lights in and out in different ways, and up and down. Other ways of modulating light include the mirrors and fill cards. Fill cards are usually placed fairly close to the object and allow us to put light into places that are too dark.

So we've got our broad lighting conditions (top and side lights on, diffusion screens in place), and now we bring in the mirrors and start placing them. We might say "Okay, let's look at this, the tonality of this spot is pretty similar to the tonality of that area on this surface and as a result they will disappear into each other - let's put a little light streak here, on that edge or surface to differentiate that place." So we swivel a mirror to make that happen. If an area is too dark in shadow and too different in tonality from the rest of the object then one uses mirrors to brighten the dark area. Textures and details are emphasized by side lighting. Hot spots are toned down to the minimum required brightness. Spend some time carefully observing what happens to the lighting on the object as you work with mirrors and fill cards. Fairly subtle effects make a significant difference in building up the image.

This is really important: it does not matter what occurs outside the viewfinder - the rectangle that is the film plane - nor how close the reflectors onto the object are. Anything can be going on out beyond the frame. You can have pieces of colored paper, fill cards, 'gobos,' mirrors, diffusers, all kinds of things as long as they are outside the frame.

### Edge lighting
We also use our mirrors for edge lighting because we generally want to have a faint, razor-thin, bright white streak at the top and sides of the object against that dark background in order to make it stand out. Again, one of the things that you have to be careful of when using mirrors like this is overdoing things and creating hot spots.

### Hot spots
Watch out for hot spots. Hot spots are easy to miss; if something is really bright, watch it, check it, tone it down. Make sure that, if you have a really bright spot, you modulate it down. With swinging mirrors, because they change position, we can modulate the degree of that hot spot quite easily.

So now we model the object, and we may say, "Oh yeah, let's put a little light streak: let's put a hot spot on here." What we're doing here is rendering, just like someone would render an object in a drawing, and we can use rendering conventions. If it's light in a particular curving stripe on a surface, then the viewer reads it as a rounded object. You can describe all kinds of forms by how you light them, and you spend some time doing it.

At a certain point it looks good, the lighting is good, there's nothing confusing when you look at the object: no wild hot spots, no unwanted shadows, the tones are different between object and ground, it looks and feels like a 3-D object (only you must remember that what you are seeing through the viewfinder is flat).

### Objective check time (wander your eyes)
Now is the time to stop and confirm what you think you are looking at. At this point, you can close your eyes a little bit if you like, make a last check and see how the main composition appears - this is your last objective check time. Now's the time that you let your eyes go loose and wander around the area, and that's when you find the hot spot on the shooting surface in the background that's bouncing off a mirror or piece of equipment that you hadn't noticed; that's when you find the little piece of paper that you hadn't spotted, or the mirror or fill card bit sticking in from one side, the blob of Fun-Tack® that's creeping out from under your object, or perhaps there's a reflective part to your object, and you are reflected in it. You need this sort of objective check time: "What's happening here?" Okay, everything's great, nothing's hanging in there, looks good; now it's almost time to take the picture.

### Depth of field check
Set the focus position one third of the way into the object. Probably set the f-stop on the lens to f-22 for maximum depth of field. Look at an out-of-focus light streak at the front and one at the rear of the object through the viewfinder. Press the depth of field preview button, check to see if the light streaks came into focus when the button was pressed. Make final decisions on f-stop, focus position and the depth of field.

### Light reading (averaging)
Aside from being tied up in the fact that they are looking at a three-dimensional object and so producing a bad image, the other main mistake people make is not averaging their light meter reading properly. For the light reading, you need to average things out. Let's say that I had an object, and it had a hot spot on it and I was using the camera through the lens metering system, and I metered from this spot, well, this spot would be the correct darkness and lightness, but everywhere else on the image would be wrong. So as we look at our object and take the light meter reading it is important to average. You don't take the reading from the part that's too dark, you don't go for the part that's too light - you average it out. And you've lit the piece so there is a balance between even tonality and hints of drama in light streaks, texture accentuation and so on.

### Where to meter from on object/ground
What I tend to do with a center weight metering system is to take a meter reading from the sides and middle of the object, and perhaps I will even lean the camera forward until the object fills the frame and make a decision about what I think is average (this is usually an excellent method providing you haven't changed the lighting conditions on the object by doing this - like having your head in the way of some of the lighting). If your head is interfering with the lighting then look in the viewfinder at the light meter reading and slowly move your head back and away from the object. You can still focus on the reading in the viewfinder from some distance off. This allows you to get your head out of the way and still check the accuracy of the meter. We could also use a gray card, slide it down in front of the object and take the reading as the light reflects off that

gray card. If your subject is overall dark or overall light use a gray card (See Collins, pp 71-79 for detailed information).

If you don't have a gray card or you have a peculiar object - perhaps it has a lot of gaps in it, so you get a lot of the dark background and there is no way you can meter off the object successfully, then take your light meter reading from the foot of the object, with one half of the center weighted circle on the object, and one half of it on that nice charcoal gray, neutral tone paper. Most of the time that will give you a successful light meter reading.

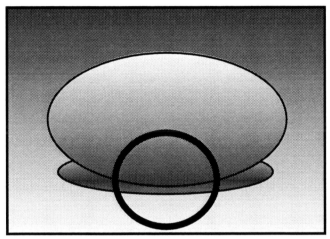

**light metering circle
positioned at base of object**

Figure 15

### Bracketing
Some words about bracketing. Professional photographers bracket; they choose the meter reading that they think is correct, based upon their experience and the light meter and so on, and then they take five shots: one at the correct meter reading and two on each side-half a stop or even sometimes a full stop each away from the f-stop that appears to be the right one, so five different f-stops, two on each side of the one you thought was right. This way you are sure to get one great shot of the object and you use this perfect shot to duplicate slides from. Note that usually it works out better for slides if you let a little less light in, if the meter says there is a not quite enough light.

The tungsten film is expensive. So I don't bracket much. I like to get 36 good shots out of 36 shots. I would say that 95% of the time that's what happens, but once in a while I screw up and ruin a roll. Most people bracket; it is wise to bracket, but if you're using the same film, and the same set-up, and you're not changing any elements of that, and you've been using it for a little while, you can begin to drop the bracketing that you do, and you can end up with adequate and good shots, most of the time. I am usually shooting 5-8 shots of the same object (because original slides are always better than duplicates and it is often cheaper to do them at once on an original roll rather than duplicating) and so get about six objects on a roll. If I bracketed I would be almost guaranteed to get six good shots from which I would then make duplicates.

You should note that for absolute perfection one does bracket. Bobby Hanson normally brackets using eight shots and has done up to twelve in order to ensure that he got a perfect shot to duplicate from. As Hanson says, each shot is only 25 cents or so and bracketing ensures a perfect image. I am however assuming that cost is a factor for you as well as having to shoot a lot of objects at once, hence my advice not to bracket once you have an established system and a feel for how it is working. Take your pick as to which approach works best for you. I must admit to bracketing when an image really must come out well.

**Take the shot**
Do a quick mental check list to see if you have thought of everything that matters. Then take the photograph. Repeat the same shot for multiples if you feel the exposure time, f-stops, focus and so on are correct. Or bracket.

# Reflective Objects

Reflective surfaces are a special case. I remember seeing an *Art in America* magazine once, and on the cover was a picture of some really famous sculptor's work in a Washington, DC gallery. It was a large, bulbous, bronze casting. It was highly polished, and what was really funny was that there on the cover of *Art in America* magazine was a picture of the sculpture, and on its surface were the photographer, the tripod, the lights, the man lying on the floor holding a large white fill card: everything in the gallery. My first thought was "These people missed this. The photographer missed it, the editors missed it, the picture selector missed it, and here it is." Reflective surfaces give you yourself back in the picture and bring the world onto the object, bring the surroundings into the image taken, which can be a real problem - it usually doesn't look good at all. Reflective surfaces tend to bring in the colors around them, which in the photo-booth as I've described it means that you get a lot of black reflections, so it looks really bad. One generally arranges to have white fill cards placed everywhere that is reflecting black to the camera until the object appears white through the viewfinder. You subtract the black reflections by using judiciously placed white reflectors until the image looks good.

One professional photographer I met, when asked by a jeweler, "So how should I make pieces best for good photographs?" said "Don't polish them." Well, real life is that we have to deal with polished objects. There are several ways of approaching this.

If you have a reflective silvery surface and it has black reflections in it you end up with a very muddy picture which has a low tonal contrast between object and background, and it really doesn't work. Hanson suggests that, instead of getting upset with the black reflections as a negative problem, you view them as a positive solution and, as described above, replace them with reflections that you actually want (usually white; rarely colored cloth or paper etc.) which to my mind is a nice way of looking at the problem.

**Tents**
The usual way of dealing with reflective objects is to shoot the object inside a translucent tent. If you have a copy stand (which is how I used to photograph most of my work when I started out) you can use it to create a vertically-oriented tent. Otherwise one constructs a situation where the object is surrounded by translucent diffusing material (Mylar®) so that no surface facing the camera is able to reflect anything except translucent or white material. One may put a large sheet of translucent material clothespinned in place over the front of the photo-booth with the camera stuck through a hole in it or a large stiff piece of white paper, card or Foam-Core® which works in the same way. The whole point is that the camera cannot see any reflections on the object from the world outside the tent. This means that we don't care about the back half of the reflective piece: only what the camera sees counts.

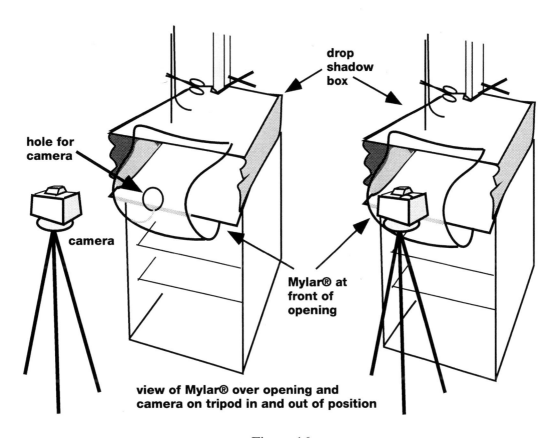

**drop shadow box**

**hole for camera**

**camera**

**Mylar® at front of opening**

**view of Mylar® over opening and camera on tripod in and out of position**

Figure 16

Another way is to take a large piece of Mylar®, and hang it over a fishing line, rod or bar and place the object inside. The more transparent the supporting part is the better: best of all is to support the Mylar® from its center with a fishing line slung over the horizontal strut above the shooting surface. Then from all sides there will be nice diffuse light, lovely white surfaces. From the front, I will still be getting the camera, and me, and all of the front of the room that the object can reflect from, and so what we do is take a large piece of white cardboard or Foam-Core®, cut a hole in the middle to stick the camera lens through so that the camera's on the back of the white card with the hole and then take the picture. In this way there will be no reflections on the object that you don't want. You want, if possible, all of the reflections on the object to be from white, translucent, or very diffusely lit surfaces. Fill cards of various shapes and pieces of translucent Mylar® all serve to replace reflections you don't want with white, neutral ones. Sometimes when shooting silver reflective geometric objects in a good light tent it can be difficult to discern the edges and corners of the object. Meltzer takes thin black paper strips and tapes them to the inside of the light tent so that they line up perfectly at the edges of the object thus defining the object's corners in a 'natural' manner for the shot. A curving black strip reflection in a rounded object may also be useful sometimes (Meltzer, p 62).

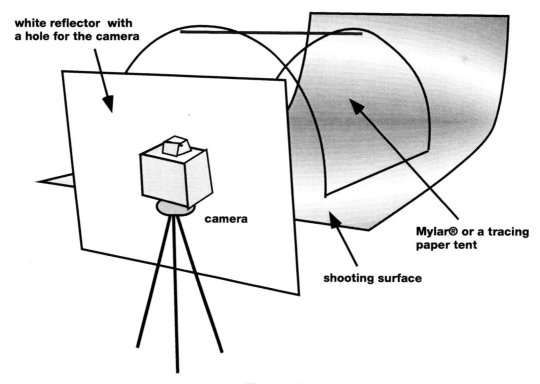

**white reflector with a hole for the camera**

**camera**

**Mylar® or a tracing paper tent**

**shooting surface**

Figure 17

Sometimes when using a tent and a white card on the front of the camera you will see the camera lens itself as a round or oval black reflection in the object. In that case slowly raise the camera on its central cranking column. Look through the lens as you do this and at a certain point the black reflection will slide out of view. At that point tighten the camera into position and take the shot.

### Copy stands

Copy stands also provide a way of dealing with reflective objects. They offer a very controllable (and hence repeatable) system for taking slides of your work. For flatter items, coins and much jewelry a copy stand is a good solution as a photo-booth system. As described before there are horizontal and vertical systems. What follows deals with a vertical system.

You can mount the camera looking straight down and create a bag suspended from the camera around the object itself so that the entire interior space is within a tent. Make sure that you fold the bag so that by releasing a single clamp (clothespin) you can quickly get a hole that is big enough to reach into and arrange the object for the shot. Note if you use a vertical set-up with a dark background cloth (black velvet) under the work that dust and any dandruff can become a real issue. When I first started out I used a pillow case; I would have the camera inside the bag, and I would point it straight down and take a picture. I would have the lights fairly close in, but I no longer recommend this approach with a pillow case, because regular cloth is laundered, and commercial laundry soaps have what's called bluing in them. Bluing is a material that fluoresces blue under normal lighting conditions. If you have a surface that is emitting a blue light, then that eliminates any yellow light that you would otherwise see. What this means is that your sheets are actually yellowish, but the bluing in them fluorescing blue eliminates the yellow, and so they appear white to us-but perhaps not to the film and camera. Instead, use white, ripstop nylon which you can buy at climbing and camping stores. This is a neutral material, it can easily be made into a bag for a vertical copy stand or stretched over frames to produce diffusion screens, and professionals really like it. It's easy to work with, inexpensive and apparently doesn't adversely affect the colors that the film records.

It is possible to make your own copy stand. I did at one point. I think my recommendation is to buy one; shop at auctions, call up print shops, printmakers, anyone who records flat items photographically and ask them if they know of any used ones. They come up regularly in my local government surplus auction center.

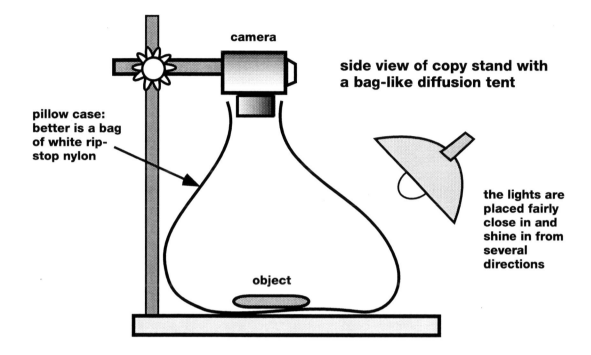

Figure 18

### Dusting (dulling) sprays

Sometimes professional photographers will use dusting sprays (also called dulling sprays) as a way of dealing with reflective objects. I don't use them myself but it might be a solution to a problem you have at some point. Dusting sprays are fine, light-colored powders in a spray can and can be bought at professional camera suppliers. I've heard of people using Arid Extra Dry® Deodorant powder in a spray can the same way. You take a highly reflective object and give it a very light coating of a fine dust, almost like the misted effect of breathing on a metal surface when it is cool and your breath condenses on it. This eliminates reflections. Then you can take the picture. Note that you don't want to make a mess or damage an object with a dulling spray so you should proceed with caution when using them. Collins only uses them on silver-colored reflective fill cards to alter the degree of reflected fill light and does not use them on objects (Collins, p 187).

When people are working with a reflective object using a dusting spray, quite often they will put the dusting spray onto the object, and then add a white 'reflection' where they think light streaks should be to describe the object to the viewer ("okay, to describe this thing, we need a white spot here and a white stripe here and a white stripe there"). One takes one's finger and wipes the dust away in a swipe where the 'reflection' should be. Then a white card is placed such that it reflects in the wiped areas, and now there are white light streaks 'where they should be' to describe the form on this less than reflective surface.

Some photographers will 'paint with light' by choosing a long exposure and hand-holding a suitable tungsten light source (I think one might be able to use a halogen flashlight - I'll have to try that sometime) while moving it rapidly back and forth or up and down to create a light streak line that follows the form of the object thus describing it in space better. I've done this once or twice but think it would work best on exposures longer than a second. Therefore, because most of the exposure times in our photo - booth are close to that, this method may not be immediately useful to you. Remember it though: it may sometime be a correct solution to a problem for you.

# Further Photography Set-up Options

**Plexiglas L's**

The use of 'Plexiglas L's' is an extremely effective small scale lighting system. You take white, translucent Plexiglas, and you make squares approximately two feet (60 cm) on each side. Then you make two L-shaped constructions by gluing the edges together. In a pinch duct tape on the outside to hold parts temporarily may be helpful. Having the L shape allows you to stack them in different ways, so that they can be instantly positioned one on another forming a top and two sides to create a perfect light tent. The object goes inside, and a white reflective card that the camera pokes through gives you a great light tent. The lights would be brought fairly close in to the translucent Plexiglas. A four-sided box can easily be made for placing an object inside and then shooting down at it. It would be lit from the sides through the Plexiglas. They can also be positioned so that the light comes up from under the object - this style of shot is used a lot with glass objects. So these Plexiglas 'Ls' give you a great deal of freedom in how you use them.

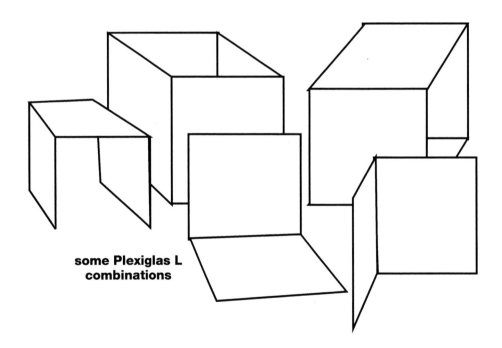

**some Plexiglas L combinations**

Figure 19

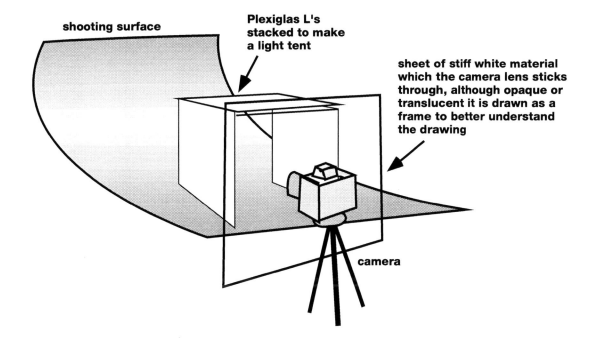

**shooting surface**

**Plexiglas L's stacked to make a light tent**

**sheet of stiff white material which the camera lens sticks through, although opaque or translucent it is drawn as a frame to better understand the drawing**

**camera**

Figure 20

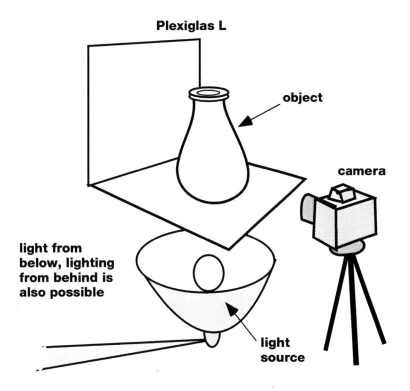

**Plexiglas L**

**object**

**camera**

**light from below, lighting from behind is also possible**

**light source**

Figure 21

An advantage of using the L as in the above diagram is that shadows cast from any overhead lighting present are eliminated because of the lighting from below.

59

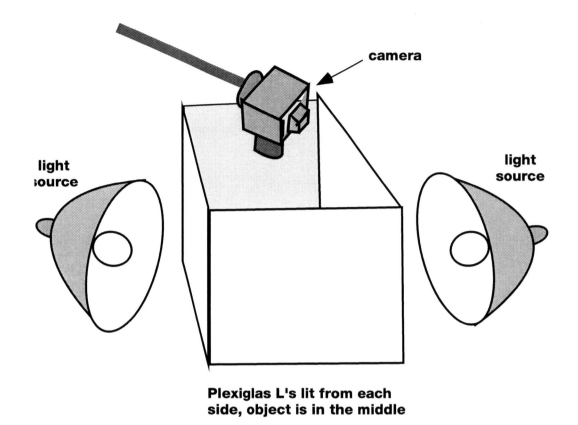

**camera**

**light source**

**light source**

**Plexiglas L's lit from each side, object is in the middle**

Figure 22

## Curving reflector card

A method that I have not used but that looks quick and easy is to take a large white curving card and stick the camera lens through it to look at the object (Bomback, p 164). If your object was particularly reflective I suspect that you would want a Mylar® 'roof' over the top of the curve to make it into more of a 'tent.' Because the curving white card fixes the camera in place you would have problems eliminating the lens reflection, but there are times I can see this as a good solution to a specific problem.

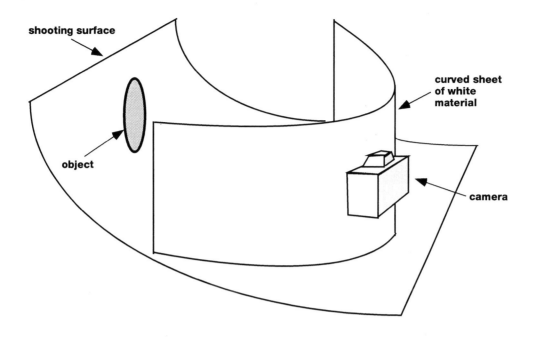

Figure 23

## Milk jugs

Another inexpensive approach for obtaining a tent is a trick using a translucent gallon (4 liter) plastic milk jug from the supermarket. Take a milk jug and cut a hole in it at the neck to receive the camera. Then cut the bottom off. Arrange the height for the correct focal distance from the lens to where you cut the bottom off, which means perhaps you have several milk jugs cut to different heights for different sizes of object. The lights are placed fairly close to the jug, or you can use daylight film and put your reflective object inside the jug outdoors to photograph it.

Figure 24

**Styrofoam cooler**

I've heard of people using a Styrofoam cooler from the grocery store as a kind of tent; you can buy them for a couple of dollars, and they work in a similar way to the milk jug, only now you've got a larger object that you stick your camera lens through. Make a round hole in the middle that is a little small for the lens (so the cooler doesn't fall off the lens if you lift it). Styrofoam coolers cut off a lot more light than a milk jug and one has to adjust for this. They're also, like all plastics, susceptible to heat so if you're using photofloods for a light source that's a potential fire hazard. Be careful of melting plastics and fumes!

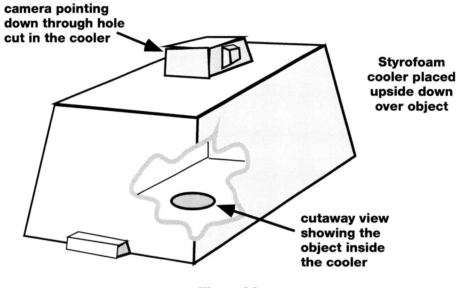

camera pointing
down through hole
cut in the cooler

Styrofoam
cooler placed
upside down
over object

cutaway view
showing the
object inside
the cooler

Figure 25

**White card on camera-shooting on the ground**

David LaPlantz once described to me a very easy solution for shooting good quality photographs of flatter objects outdoors using daylight film. You take a big white card or Foam-Core® (about 2-3 feet square) with the camera lens stuck through a hole in the middle of it and place your shooting surface on the ground outside. You stand leaning over the object which is in the middle of the shooting surface. The light comes in from the sides, bounces back off the ground and the edges of the shooting surface, hits the white underside of the sheet the camera is stuck through, and then bounces back down to the object providing front and side lighting for it with a very smooth and even, nice, white light. I've seen some photographs done like this that you would swear had to have been done on a more complex system. It is best for flatter objects. You have to have good sunlight, and you have to be bouncing the light off surfaces before it reaches your object. This is a good place for shooting surfaces like Color-Aid® paper - papers that are graduated, so they go from one tone to another. Pantone® is another maker of background papers. I've seen a slide done on this set-up where the object was just sitting on a very beautiful, graduated-tone, colored paper surface, and it looked like it was sitting on a piece of invisible glass and magically floating some distance in front of a drop shadow background.

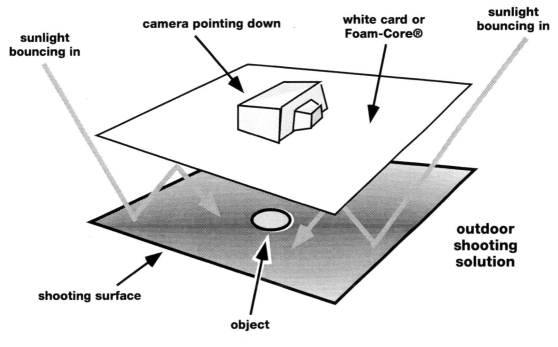

Figure 26

# Working with 35 mm Slides

### Getting slides developed

A note on slide developing: you want your slides to be developed for the best quality possible. If you want to impress your local photo shop, you go in and you ask "do you do dip and dunk E-6 photo processing?" Dip and dunk means that it's not touched by human hands or rollers or anything, and it's supposed to be a much better quality of developing. E-6, which is the standard slide processing used for the films we've been discussing, can normally be done in a one-hour photo shop, but in a one-hour photo shop you may run into old chemicals (I've seen this), you may run into scratches from dirt on the rollers (I've seen this), so one-hour photo shops are not generally great unless you have developed a relationship with the owner where you can say "Are the chemicals fresh? Is the machine operating well?" and if you've done that, they're usually fine. Ask where your top local art college or university photography students take their slides for E-6 processing and you will usually find a good processor at a reasonable cost.

The other way to guarantee that you'll get good results in the developing of your slides is to connect with somebody who has their own film in the same tank, because then they've got their own stuff on the line. This means finding a local studio photographer who does magazine shots and so on, who does E-6 regularly, and asking if you can pay to have your film developed along with theirs. They have a commitment to their film, and they'll take good care of yours too.

Another good source is teaching hospitals, and dental faculties, because medical people like top-quality results, and they do E-6 processing of pathology slides all the time, so if you can connect with a hospital or a teaching faculty, and have your things developed along with them, that's usually a good way to go as well.

Then there are the professional labs you can find in the yellow pages of the phone book. Best is to get recommendations from several photographers until you hear the same lab mentioned a couple of times. You will pay a little more but it should be 'dip and dunk' processing and should be good quality. That said, I've had scratches and bad chemicals from professional labs as well.

## Glass mounts

It is very important to consider having glass mounts for your slides, At the very least for your permanent slide set (two such sets is better). The mounts I like are called Gepe® mounts, and they can be bought at any standard photo shop for about 50 cents each. Note: that permanent set never leaves you.

A couple of words on glass mounts: if you are like me, when you start taking pictures you don't bother with glass mounting them, and after awhile, you end up with thousands of slides, and it's just such a horrendous job to even imagine going and glass mounting them that you don't do it. So go one better on me and glass mount them like mad right away when you start producing good slides.

## Permanent slide set

I recommend that, as you begin taking pictures, you glass mount at least one permanent set of slides. You keep your permanent set well organized, labeled and stored. Only duplicate slides leave you. Any time that you send a slide out, count on not getting it back. If you get it back, life is good, but just count that it's a goner. If you're really fanatic, you have a second permanent set, and this permanent set is sent to a slide archiving place. At this slide archiving company the temperature and humidity are controlled and the slides are stored in the dark because any exposure to light will alter your slides: all in order to keep them stable.

## Slide longevity

What occurs with slides is that they have a color life span of about 15 years - 15 to 20 years depending upon what you do - and every time you put them in a projector they die a little more. So, if you are developing a career in the arts, and you're going to be at this for 30 or 40 years, you know that your slides aren't going to last. Some people will then archive their slides, and as their current slides begin to die, they go back to the archiving place, they pull them out, make dupes from them and continue. It is very important to have some slide sets around that you can use for your posterity as an artist or craftsperson.

Collins says Kodachrome has the best longevity, but fades fastest on projection. He also says that Fujichrome has superior stability for projection but only average dye stability and tends to stain formation (yellowish staining which forms with time). Ektachrome tends to stain formation even when stored in the dark (Collins, p 62).

One interesting storage alternative available now is to get a very high-resolution digitized image made of a slide-then it can't change unless you lose your computer storage media and it can be output as a 35 mm slide for projection again at a quality near that of the original. It is quite inexpensive to have your slides scanned to a photo CD.

## Handling Slides

If your slides are not glass mounted avoid touching the film, only hold them by the edges. Dust can be removed with a canned dry air spray from a photo store (use from a distance) or gentle brushing with a sable watercolor brush. A rapid flick with a fingernail on the outside edge of a slide mount can dislodge dust pretty effectively - just watch out for flicking your slide across the room. If you have fingerprints on the film side (the shiny side) you can wipe them off gently with Kodak film cleaner or ether (danger!!). If fingerprints are on the emulsion side Meltzer suggests unmounting the slide, then a soaking diluted Photo-Flo® for a time, rinsing and remounting. Use cotton gloves when touching negatives (Meltzer, p 108).

## Labeling slides

I prefer glass mounts first, then plastic mounts, lastly cardboard. When you have a slide duplicated specify whether you want plastic or cardboard mounts. Don't ask a lab to glass mount slides for you; it is far cheaper to do it yourself and is not difficult to do. I've seen at least one competition that specified slides in cardboard mounts but it is very easy to unmount a slide from a plastic mount and install it into a cardboard one from a photography supplier.

A slide should have a little red dot on the lower left-hand corner. The red dot is on the front of the slide, that is, on the side of the slide where text is legible or the image is the right way around. When the slides are loaded in a carousel the red dot will be upwards and show from the back of the projector so the presenter knows they have the slide upside down and thus oriented correctly for viewing. If I have a slide presentation with left and right carousels then I number every slide and use a permanent marker dot (red for left, green for right) on the slide next to the number. I also run a red or green magic marker along the bottoms of the slides when they are mounted in the carousel so that I know if all the rights and lefts are together when I look at the loaded carousel.

Using a black permanent marker, draw a little arrow in the top right hand corner of the slide to show which way is up for people who will be looking at the slide in a slide sheet or not projected. Put labels on each slide listing your name, title, materials, size, date of the work.

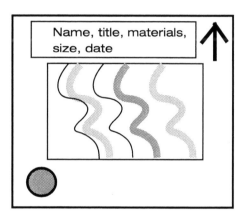

Figure 27

I use a laser printer to print slide labels at a very small point size onto peel-and-stick sheet label material, then cut the labels out and stick them on. This is rapid and easy. I have heard of people using those inexpensive peel-and-stick address labels that one often gets coupons for in junk mail. One has the slide label text done instead of an address and then has 250 labels for the same slide. This approach is obviously best if you are doing a lot of the same image.

## Storing slides

Do not use PVC slide pages, use polypropylene or Kimac®. Do not stack slide pages on top of one another in a horizontal pile as it damages the slides, use vertical binders instead. They should be in a cool, dark place with air circulation (Meltzer, p 109). Try and avoid regular cardboard boxes or paper in the same cupboard as the slides because they outgas acid (a result of how most papers are made). An option I like is to use a metal filing cabinet and hanging files for storage. You buy the hanging files, cut almost all of the paper folder portion off and discard it leaving a thin strip with the hooks intact. The plastic slide page gets stapled to this and then the slides hang vertically in their slide pages. Each hanging file folder then makes two hanging slide pages.

Mostly, though, I store my slides in the dark in their original plastic boxes and label the ends of the boxes by subject so I can pull slides of certain objects out quickly. Several companies are mentioned later in regard to professional slide archiving, storage and presentation supplies.

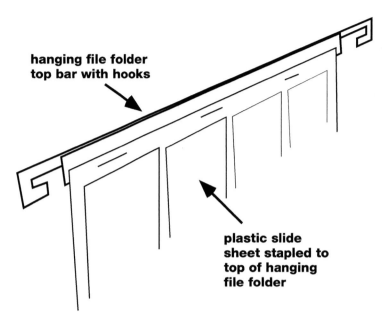

**hanging file folder top bar with hooks**

**plastic slide sheet stapled to top of hanging file folder**

Figure 28

### Projecting slides

Here are several hints for projecting slides. We are assuming you are doing a presentation with them. Don't project originals unless you have to: use duplicates. Always have on hand a back-up projector, 2 extra bulbs, an extension cord and an extra carousel (voice of experience). Use 80-slide carousels (the 140 s often tend to jam, wrecking your slide in the process). If a carousel jams there is a quick release lever at the center; you will have to use a coin (a quarter) to open older carousels. Always check the retaining ring to see if it is tight. Always run through the slides in the space where you are going to show them beforehand several times so you have a sense of the space and can pick out any backwards slides, upside down ones and so on. Never apologize for a bad slide, just keep on going.

Don't use cardboard mounts in British slide projectors (they have a stronger spring than North American ones and destroy your slides by slamming them up against the retaining ring - they are built for glass mounts and heavier mounts than are common in North America). Try not to hold a slide on the screen too long (as light kills your slides).

Laser pointers are great and can be had for less than $40.00 at this point. Don't overuse them but careful use adds a great deal to a slide presentation. If you ever want to really impress people at large academic conferences take along a small, good pair of opera glasses to look at the details on slides projected at the front of the room - this proves you know what you are doing.

### Digital Work

Digital photography is really cool and to get usable quality in 1997, really expensive. If you need digital images have them scanned in from slides at a service bureau or professional photo lab (they all do digital work now). A less expensive option is to have a regular photo store put them on a Kodak photo CD for you. This runs between $1.50 and $2.00 per image at this point and you can fit somewhere between 60 and 100 images onto one CD. A dedicated slide scanner is quite expensive at the moment but you can get a high DPI resolution flatbed scanner with a transparency adapter which allows you to scan in slides, print photos and large format transparencies as well.

It is possible to scan a fairly flat or low-relief object right on a standard flatbed scanner and, in the case of jewelry at least, get very nice results which can be used to create on-screen slide shows (Lyn Strelau, a Calgary goldsmith, does this to good effect to show his customers his work). Architectural scanners work as well and one can successfully scan surprisingly three-dimensional objects on them.

Once the image is digitized it can be manipulated in a program like Photoshop. This has interesting implications for jurying of objects by using slides. There is already a long history of preparing objects just for a photograph or of retouching a photograph to 'improve' an image. I remember a teacher of mine who I questioned about his use of a delicate sandblasted finish on a piece of gold jewelry (which I felt would not last five minutes when worn by a customer). At the time I was shocked when he said "It only has to hold up for the photograph." A couple of years ago there were rumors among jewelers doing the large US craft fairs that some people had been juried into shows based on slides of non-existent work, that is, jewelry that was literally glued together for the shot, was made in precious materials but was not actually a functional piece of jewelry except for the purposes of photography. Digitized images are eminently manipulatable. Juries and arts and crafts organizations have not yet faced up to the implications of being able to easily output a slide of an enhanced piece or to 'repair' problems on the slide that the object itself has.

There are various standard formats used for digitized images: EPS and TIF are common ones. JPEG is a compression format that is used extensively on the World Wide Web (internet) because image memory requirements can be really tiny and still give an acceptable image on a computer screen (approximately 72 DPI resolution). Try and print it out, however, and you will see what a rough thing a small JPEG image really is. But if you want images on a CDROM or on a web site then JPEGs are great. Another interesting thing is that because they are so small it is possible to put some 50 or more onto an ordinary floppy disc that costs fifty cents, and as long as a recipient has an internet browser program, Photoshop or a JPEG viewer, they can see your images. This provides an incredibly inexpensive way of distributing images for people to look at.

If you are interested in digital photography talk to your local newspaper photographers (who are going digital faster than anyone else), do research and read magazines for awhile to get a sense of things before leaping into spending money on equipment and software.

# Considerations in Photographing Various Media

Three-dimensional objects will be well served by the methods described earlier in the book, such as overhead diffuse lighting, fill card and mirror use. For flat things (like prints) use copy set-ups which primarily consist of extremely even light on the object and the camera centered properly on the work. Shiny things will need tents. We did, however, ask a number of craftspeople and artists whether there were any special considerations they felt were associated with different media. The following is derived from their comments.

**Paper and flat art**
Sue Archer and Georgia Deal made these points: It is important in dealing with paper to retain some sense of relief and surface texture. This could be accomplished by varying the light distances a bit or adding a side lighting source to the copy set-up. Color saturation is a tricky one

and you will just have to experiment. Try Kodachrome to see if you like it any better than the tungsten films. In large objects in order to shoot the whole thing you may lose a sense of detail and so have to provide both a global shot of the object and several detailed shots as well. You will have to choose a compromise: color, bold graphic quality versus a sense of detail.

## Textiles
Layne Goldsmith and Akemi Nakano Cohn contributed some thoughts. For textiles and quilts that are flat the considerations are similar. A sense of texture is very important and so side lighting helps. A raking light at about 30 degrees, from one side with a fill card on the shadow side can produce good results with a quilt (Collins, p 96). Lyn Pflueger, a Calgary fiber artist, says that because textiles, unlike metal, are non-reflective, they tend to 'suck up' light, so lighting is a problem. It's very easy to get an image that is too dark, or not sharp and clear enough. This can be remedied by lighting the surface strongly, using a gray card and bracketing. Presentation and display for the photograph is also a concern; hanging textile pieces on the wall is often convenient, but is not always the best solution because then you lose the sense of three-dimensionality that some pieces have. Tapestries can have relief parts in otherwise flat work. Again, some cross lighting can be helpful. Here's where mirrors are useful with their ability to spotlight specific areas on a piece.

## Baskets
In regard to baskets Lissa Hunter and Crys Harse had the following comments. Depth of field is important, especially for larger pieces needing some 12-15" depth of field. One may need to increase the general lighting levels or begin to use exposures longer than 1 second. If you are getting a camera for such objects then you might want a camera that has settings for longer time periods than a second. Depth of field is important for woven pieces where specific weaves matter. This is because structure is very important to basket makers. Therefore with baskets it is important to take good detail shots of the surfaces and structures occurring. There is some concern about trying to convey the intimate, tactile, close understanding of the material and process experienced by the maker.

Harse also wants a background light enough to translate well into both black and white slides and prints or even black and white laser prints. My suggestion would be to try a white shooting surface and work with the lighting to obtain a drop shadow effect. Texture and its subtleties are of importance as well. It would therefore be good to use side lighting and miniature spotlighting with mirrors and perhaps judicious projector use as well. Fill lighting is very important to lighten shadowed areas. Be careful of what shadows are doing on the object and background.

Another theme very important to basket makers (and to many people who make vessels) is the play of inside and out and what that means. Therefore position the camera so you can see some of the inside of the object to better describe it (a vertical shot for instance at 45 degrees downwards towards the object).

## Ceramics
In regard to ceramics we asked Barbara Tipton and Peter Beasecker for some comments. As someone who publishes a ceramicists magazine, Tipton finds that most problems with submitted photos stem from ceramicists hiring photographers who are versed primarily in 2-dimensional objects, when specialized product photographers would be more familiar with 3-D work. Depth of field is important, and the ability to show surface textures. So, side lighting, long exposures, mirrors. The degree of glare and reflection is very important in indicating a particular quality of surface or glaze. This means side lighting and spotlighting to reveal those qualities. Watch out for hot spots. Beasecker tones down a hot spot by blotting the surface with beeswax (I'd avoid this on

some porous or textured surfaces). Broad soft box lighting from above along with fill cards works well with many ceramics so that one is reflecting light back upwards against the object from the sides. Dealing with portraying the scale of work: its size can be a difficult thing and a concern. Inserting a penny or a ruler to indicate scale is simply not done any more. An additional shot of the artist at work in the studio along with the object can be a good way to indicate scale. Tipton had some concern about people using the correct film types. Regarding composition of photos sent in for publication: for technical reasons, leave enough background space around the object.

## Jewelry

Because jewelry is the focus of most of my own photography, the approaches I've said I use personally throughout the text work well for most jewelry objects. Coins work well with side lighting of various kinds; experiment also with altering the distance of various lights from the coin.

## Wood

Henry Schlosser was our consultant for wood. He emphasized documentary, rather than 'artistic' photographs (it's that 'neutral background is better' again). Magazines like an unobtrusive background so the object itself is the focus of the picture. He noted problems with hot spots and fill lighting. Good lighting is very important because colors tend to be very subtle, and you want to be able to make out different colors. You might experiment again with film types here. An issue he noted too is one that sometimes occurs when photographing paintings: 'false color.' The film records a different color than you see: i.e. a white wood appears green in the photograph. Collins suggests that using a UV and/or an Infrared filter or even UV filter material over the lights may help this as the color differences are caused by the material fluorescing under excitation of the UV or infrared light being emitted by the photofloods. He has filter suggestions to compensate for this as well but notes it is a very complex subject (Collins, pp 66-67). For reproduction, Schlosser notes that magazines want fairly high contrast photos - sharp and 'crisp.'

## Models

We asked Morgan B. Turney, the editor of Canadian Railway Modeller, for some comments. His largest concern in model photography is depth of field - specifically, what type of lens to use with an SLR camera to get good depth of field. Again we generally get greater depth of field by playing with lighting levels, small f-stops and long exposures. Mirrors for modeling light on the objects would be useful. Detail, texture and color are of importance.

Mr. Turney himself uses a 28 mm lens with 2x extenders to make an f-stop of 22 into one of 45, then cuts the exposure time in half to produce a good close-up with good depth of field. Hmm, sounds like he knows what he's doing - I refer model makers with further questions not answered in this book to your respective journals.

## Glass

Many professional photographers cringe when someone brings them a glass object to shoot.

Transparency, hot spots, reflection, color are all special issues with glass. Plexiglas L's provide some good options for glass. Glass seems to work well when lit from below, from the sides or above through a diffusion screen or translucent white Plexiglas or frosted glass. You might try a tent. Defining edges with thin light streaks would come from fill cards and side lighting. One can cut out translucent Mylar® or white paper in the shape of the object and place it behind the glass to deal with the transparency problem as long as it doesn't distort the understanding of your object. A couple of set-ups that have been used for glass follow (from Bomback, p 160).

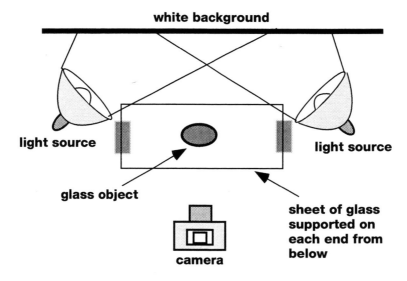

Figure 29

A similar approach produces quite different effects when the glass is lit from the sides (and possibly from below as well) in front of a black background (Meltzer, p 69). This lights the edges and any details within the glass. I don't use this approach but there may be a time when this will be a good solution for you, perhaps with paper-weights or rock crystals.

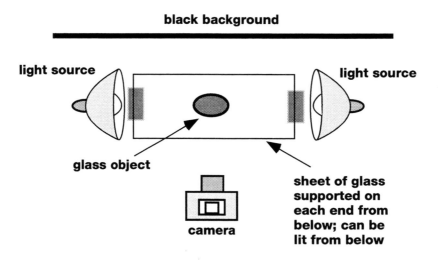

Figure 30

# What to Do with Photos Now That You Have Them

As a photographer taking pictures of objects you have made you are actively documenting your work. Taking the photographs is, however, only one part of effectively documenting your activity as an artist. The next sections will speak of the broader documentation and professional activities necessary for success in your field. Photographs and images are an integral part of this public relations work, networking and sharing of visual ideas with your community that is all part of being a professional.

**Some PR tools to have on your side**
Parts of the following text were previously published in the book *Shareware* (Brain Press).

The point is to survive and prosper as an artist or craftsperson. This means that one has to deal with the basics of running a small business, independent contracting, contracts and marketing. It is the marketing that feeds one as no amount of wonderful art work will pay the rent and purchase materials unless it has a market. This does not mean one panders to taste - on the contrary one is as true to oneself and one's art as possible and only has to find the correct audience for it that will pay to allow one to do what one wants. This is true whether one is applying for grants, making wildly esoteric conceptual art, landscape painting or creating sculpture and objects in a so-called craft media. This means that you have to document by creating images, by generating photographs and text about what you do.

To generate written documents in support of your professional activity it is important to have and use a computer - I recommend a Macintosh as easiest to learn. A computer turns information into chunks you can copy, blend and recombine easily to create different kinds of documents to support your marketing efforts. It is also very important to have a fax machine. They are less than $200.00 now and expand your ability to interact with the rest of the world in very interesting ways. The time saved by not having to run around taking things to fax is worth a lot. The perceived professionalism on your part and the copy function that most machines have is useful too. I recommend a separate fax line on which you also have your internet connection to your computer (yes, I think these things are useful). A fax machine hooked up like this also lets you fax things into your computer as a crude sort of scanner.

To publish and send out press releases and appear in magazines is not an ego trip or arrogant behavior - it is a method of communication, of sharing information and views, of discourse. According to national surveys in the arts and crafts, a lack of business and marketing skills is the number one problem cited by artists and craftspeople as hindering their careers.

Remember too that no one does this stuff for you - you have to do it for yourself (or subcontract it).

From what I've observed among 'successful' artists, it seems that to document yourself thoroughly and frequently in the culture has some interesting potential effects. You do not have to compromise the work, merely to document what you are doing anyway. Documentation gives people the 'cultural handles' they can use to make money on you, then you get to go along for the ride busily making whatever it is you want to and earning a living from the people in the art business who are making money on you and your cultural image. Give the people who are disposed to making money the tools to do it with you. This means a commitment of time to one's own PR project, probably the equivalent of an hour a week but which often seems to occur in several-day bursts during the year. I should also point out that I am no paragon of virtue with proper use of PR opportunities, merely that the comments here reflect my observations of what seems to work, as well as my experience.

There are some things one sends out constantly: biographies of various lengths, statements on one's work of various lengths, black and white photos, slides and a resumé. Photocopies of articles or catalogues are good. Postcards or color prints of work can be useful.

The main principle in dealing with PR materials is to do as much work for the recipient as possible so they don't have to struggle to deal with you or your supplied materials and you thus fit easily into their lives and what they are doing. Give them the tools to sell you in their own self-interest and they will do so. Do the work for people and they will value you. Be available on an instant to supply people with information and images. This means keeping current press kits and photographic documentation. It means acting professionally and carrying out most of what you begin.

### Participation

Simply participating by having images available is probably 80% of getting published. A friend of mine once had a piece appear on the cover of *American Craft*. Various people mentioned to him his supposed influence with editors, when he hadn't done anything special to get it on the cover. So he called them up and asked why they had chosen his piece. They said "You're the only one who sent a picture." I've heard variations on this theme a number of times. You would be surprised how few people actually get down to taking care of their PR project and having images available to share with their field. Just being available and accommodating is often enough.

### Biography

A good one is hard to do. The most difficult thing to learn is to distance yourself so you can talk about yourself in the third person and look at yourself objectively, avoiding all the small internal put downs one may have and noticing that you (and everyone) has accomplishments or experiences that are unique and interesting. With bios and statements the writing should be interesting so that if you were reading it as someone else's, you would want to keep on reading, want to read to the end. It is a story about someone-and a good one. Different lengths are necessary. In general start with a big one of a page and a half or so and then boil down to different-sized paragraphs on down to a two-or three - sentence one. I put all mine on one sheet, some people keep them separate. You will need to review and revise your biographies once every two years or so.

### Statements

Sometimes people will write a biography as if it is a statement so check your earlier biographies for clues as to what may belong in your statement. A statement is about what you believe in, what is important to you, what positions you take, what drives your art work, what your stand is in the world and on your art. A one-paragraph statement, a half-a-page and a full-page one will suffice. To write one check your sketch books for notes you have written to yourself about your beliefs or spend some time with a friend talking about what you believe in and what is important to you - and take notes. Review/revise statements once a year.

### Resumé

A resumé may be one page and is a maximum of two pages. Usually organized in point form with a reverse chronology (latest date first), it lists accomplishments and recognitions and is evidence of professional activity such as an exhibition record. Update once a year. More detail on writing a resumé appears later.

### Black and White Photos

You need black and white photos of your work because they lend validity to your work and get published. Color slides and photos almost never get published - black and white does. If you really turn someone on with your work they will come after you for color shots or send their own photographer. If you send a B/W of work out with every press release you should get published about one out of five times simply because no one else will have done it and they need filler for the newspaper.

Of course your work could be brilliant enough to make it on its own merits but my experience is that it is not validity that makes for publication but mere willingness to participate on this level - and having your photos there when they need them. I think it is important to know how to do black and white printing to keep your overhead costs down. Digital cameras and photography will make that computer of yours into your own darkroom system pretty soon, so that black and whites will be generated (already half-toned for printing) from a computer.

I have color postcards made of my work regularly. Postcards have the advantage of being already half-tone screened so that they serve admirably for publication in newspapers as black and white images - a fact that may need pointing out to the recipient. I suggest making 6-10 prints of every image you produce. This means choosing your images carefully for maximum use and application. I always print onto 8"x10" photographic paper cut in two to make two 4" x5"prints. I print so as to leave a thick white border in one place on the paper. This is because I then type my last name and the description of the photo on the back of the photo behind the white space around the edges. If you have written behind the picture area this can interfere with reproducing the photo. Some people use a pencil instead to allow removal of the text and to keep ink from rubbing off onto other photographs in a pile. Indicate the top of the photo with an arrow on the back and write "up" next to the arrow to make sure. Remember to make things as easy as possible for the recipient. I usually place each black and white in a folded sheet of white paper as a sleeve to keep it clean and nice. Of course, always ship photos in a sturdy envelope (I like the ripstop stuff) with a cardboard stiffener in it to keep the photos from being bent. Address and write on the envelope before putting the photographs in - this will keep you from accidentally damaging the photo inside (Meltzer, p 90). Label the envelope 'PHOTOS - DO NOT BEND' as validations and to keep them more intact.

Never expect to get photos - or anything you mail out - back. Including stamped, self - addressed envelopes is a good insurance policy, but assume you will never see them again and you won't be disappointed, just happy when some do come back. Black and whites can be made from color slides though there is an increase in contrast. Black and white film can also be used to copy from color prints. It is important to have black and white self portraits, like a portrait or of you working at your art. Print a ton of these: my experience is that it is a long time until you get around to this job again. A new option is to use Ilford XP2 400 ISO film which produces black and white prints with the standard C41 color printing process used everywhere for making color prints.

### Color Images
Color images lend an odd validity to an image, more so than black and white. Slides should be properly labeled. Color prints are sometimes useful and are inexpensive. Slides can be taken from color prints on a copy stand. Color stickers of photographs can be made (Photolabels USA). Color photocopies offer good opportunities and can be made from slides or prints. Postcards are very cost-effective per unit to give away. European galleries apparently like to see portfolios of color prints rather than slides. A new option is a desktop photo printer for a computer. These let you print good quality color 'photographs' from images you have digitized. Currently about $400.00, the price on these will sink rapidly.

### Overruns
If you are having something printed, say a page in a catalog or a whole catalog for a show, an invitation, an article in a magazine, whatever is being printed, always ask for an overrun. Once the press is set to print the item anyway it is only pennies to keep on printing to make extras in high quality for far less than you could ever have them done on your own. I usually ask for an overrun of 250 which lasts for about ten years of careful dispensing. My experience is that one is often not charged for it simply because so few people ask for an overrun.

### Press Kits
Experienced artists may keep several versions of a press kit ready to go at any time. A friend of mine has several levels of press kit. A simple introduction kit has some photocopies of articles

about him, postcards and bio. A second level has more information, a black and white or so, color images, more photocopies of articles, reviews and so on. There are up to twenty of these ready to go at any time. They are reviewed and revised once every three months. Another level has in addition a catalog, quality color images and black and whites, quality reproductions - tins and attractive special inserts. Only 3 or so sets of the top level are kept and they are reviewed and revised monthly. This readiness has paid off for him a number of times. A press kit should contain items from the preceding categories.

### Press Releases

There must be a 'hook,' a reason why it should be published: you got in an exhibition, won a prize, did this or that of interest and currency. It must be readable and interesting - whatever you would want to keep reading. There should be an intriguing headline to the dated release. The first paragraph should contain the traditional 'Who, What, When, Where, Why.' Subsequent paragraphs should be separated by white space from the first (and from each other) and be in descending order of information ending with biographical information about you and an exhortation to contact you for further information. The paragraphs are designed to read well and also to be usable in additive chunks so that at the end of the day the newspaper or magazine wanting to fill holes in the body text can do so easily and in a modular way (adding any paragraph in order, still making sense) up to the whole press release. Again, you are doing the work for the recipient so they can easily use it to solve their problems of space to fill or information to pass on. Sending out B/Ws is not a bad idea if your 'hook' is good enough. Up to half may make it into magazines and newspapers which is a lot better than when one just sends a press release out.

### Networking

This is all kinds of things, from keeping up with magazines in your field to writing letters, going to conferences and meetings, contributing artistically in a volunteer manner to your community, exhibiting in group shows, going to openings and so on. It is about putting yourself in the way of information; of being well-informed about your field and the arts. It results in connections - people are social and they look for patterns, they look for categories to fit you into. Being available and a part of things makes it more likely that one of the people you come into contact with can make a connection involving you. As an artist this results in new and varied options.

### Longevity

Persistence and hard work is worth more than raw talent as an artist. I've seen brilliant stars burn out and leave the field or be unable to function as artists and to make their living from it. I've also seen artists who got there by sheer practice and hard work, whose early work was problematic but who became really good artists given time and persistence. Research and ongoing learning are part of this as well. A commitment to the field will usually result in personal success. Creating ripples in the culture, documenting one's activity in this life is, however, part of financial success in the field.

### Resumés and approaching galleries

The first questions to ask yourself when preparing a resumé are: For whom is it intended? What do I want it to represent? Applying for a zoo keeper's job you might put down your experience carrying llamas across the Andes but you would probably leave it out when applying for a position as a welder. For galleries you should have information they will be interested in: previous exhibitions, articles on your work and so on that serve to establish you as a serious artist/craftsperson in their eyes.

There are various ways of organizing the information to be presented. When initially contacting a gallery the resumé should ideally be one page for ease of reading. Therefore only the information most relevant to the gallery owner is used. It is usual to have information listed in reverse chronological order, that is, with the most recent item first. One would thus have several lines on education, exhibitions, awards, articles on your work and if there is any room left a line or so on work experience if necessary. Point form is an approach which lists your strong points first, followed by the events that back up the strong points you have listed.

The resumé, photocopies etc. serve as an accompaniment to the carefully done letter of inquiry personally addressed to the art gallery director or owner (no "Dear Sirs" letters). It may touch on one's intentions in the work, reasons for seeking representation at that particular gallery or, more pragmatically, one's prices for work. It may be useful to mention benefits both to the gallery and to yourself at some point in the letter.

This might be accompanied by photocopies of important articles about you or your work. If you have postcards of your work, or exhibition catalogs available, they should be included.

The package is a 'throwaway' and serves as an introduction to the gallery. If the gallery is interested in seeing slides they will contact you using a stamped, self-addressed postcard which you included that has a check box for 'would like to see slides.' By keeping the package's weight down one saves money in the long run by sending slides out only to those galleries really interested in seeing ones work. If asked to (or if you like, even on the initial contact to the gallery) you can send an entire presentation package to the gallery.

The labeled slides, together with a page of numbered slide descriptions, go in another polypropylene or vinyl binder. All this looks slick, lets you put less cramped information about each slide on the accompanying sheet and allows the viewer to read about the slides while using a projector.

A possible resumé organization for presentation to a gallery is:
Name and address at the top, telephone number, fax number, Email address
Birthdate (if you feel it necessary)
**Education** (all dated items most recent first)
Formal art education, academic education, apprenticeship, work-study programs
**One-Person Shows**
Include date, gallery name, city, country
**Juried Exhibitions and Group Shows**
Student exhibitions - if appropriate
**Awards and Grants**
**Work in Collections**
**Articles about the Applicant** (include newspaper articles)
Author's last name, first name; article title, magazine or newspaper (underlined),    pages, date
**Work Experience**
**Travel** (if appropriate), **Languages** (if appropriate)
**Special skills or interests** (if appropriate)
i.e. Something the gallery owner can interest customers with: ". . . and the artist collects poisonous snakes in their spare time."

If you don't have a computer and a laser printer or access to one it is a very good idea to pay for a professional typist to type your resumé, as they are familiar with print conventions, make few mistakes and have a professional-quality word processor and laser printer which lends an air of respectability to even a small resumé. Any photocopies made of it should be done on the best quality copier available as the grainy, smeared copies so often produced from over-used equipment detract from a resumé. The resumé should be in an acetate or vinyl report binder to protect it and to add to the presentation. Any time I put a presentation involving more than about ten pages together I start using tabs to help the reader find parts more easily.

Photocopies of important articles may be included as may some black and white glossy prints (5" x 4" min.) for the gallery to use in publicity should they decide to use your work. I have color postcards of my work made every year and because they are cheap per unit I can include color pictures of my work in every package. Color lends a curious validity to one's work. Postcards have the advantage of being already half-tone screened so that they serve admirably for publication in newspapers - a fact that may need pointing out to the recipient. If one makes postcards regularly then one can offer 500 or a thousand cards free to a gallery as exhibition announcements as an incentive. Of course, maybe you will get them done by the gallery for free or be able to go halves on a card for a specific show. Always ask for an overrun with such printings.

Finally, you should include return postage. This gives a professional effect (you often get the stamps back) and is a bit of insurance for getting your slides back.

All this is a guide, not the only way to do things. However, the better your presentation, the more seriously galleries will take you and the better your results. This holds especially true when applying for an exhibition in a gallery.

### A Gallery Contact Check List

- Personal letter to the director or curator. Letterhead is good but not essential. A nice presentation helps.

- Strong re-usable packaging, preferably with peel-and-stick return address labels enclosed or a stamped, self-addressed envelope for the return of materials folded up and enclosed in your contact envelope. Make it easy for people to deal with you: do the work for them.

- Return postage for the package, labeled for easy return to you. International postal coupons can be bought when you mail a package to another country and this allows the recipient to cash them in for the return postage.

- Good binding system for your presentation: think quality and professionalism, put yourself in their shoes in terms of what would impress you. Think about details and let it show that you have thought about every layered detail of the package, that you are behaving as a professional artist and so should be treated as one.

- Slide page of 20 slides and descriptions.

- Short 1 or 2 page resumé and possibly a full C.V. (not if it is over 10 pages or so).

- Biography: I provide various options in different lengths to make it easy for people.

- Statement on work. Some people provide them in different lengths.

- Photocopies of articles or reviews or catalog introductions that mention you. If none are available then letters of reference from teachers or a page of quotes by others (the better known they are the better) about the quality of your work is useful.

- B/W photos, 1-2. Offer to provide more B/Ws or a B/W self-portrait upon request.

- Color photocopies of slides, or prints, postcards, color photolabels or other color images

### Press Kit contents to accompany a press release

- Press release, introductory note addressed to the individual you want to reach; some people invite reporters or editors out for a coffee meeting (and pay for it).

- Make everything easy to read and understand.

- Good presentation: think quality and professionalism, put yourself in their shoes in terms of what would impress you. Think about details and let it show that you are a professional.

- A short chunk of biography is included in the press release, as is a contact phone or fax number for people to reach you. Some media people prefer faxing as it is less work to get the information.

- Photocopy of an article or reviews about you, yellow highlighter marker over your name or, as I do, on the left hand margin where you are mentioned is useful. News people only have a second or so to look at your presentation before they make a decision to throw it away or use it. Quotes by others (the better known they are the better) about the quality of your work are useful here.

- B/W photo. Think drama, glossy, good grays and tonal range, not too contrasty: what would you want to see if you were looking at a magazine or newspaper? What would tickle your fancy?

- Color photocopy of a slide or a postcard. As you won't get anything back don't invest much money in this one - this is where postcards become cost-effective.

**Some useful addresses for self-promotion**

This is a list of addresses I have found useful for 'PR tools,' printing, slide duplication, photo stickers, archival slide pages and so on. Each address is followed by a short comment on their services. Note that this list by no means covers all the possible sources. More sources are given at the end of the book. Any prices given can only be considered a rough guide and will change with time.

There are many books and publications available which can assist in learning how to go about promotion. Check with your local business and journalism faculties for information. Craft organizations and publications are also sources for this information. Thomas Mann and Libby Platus among others offer superb workshops on professionalism and use of PR tools. Jay Levinson and Seth Godin's Guerrilla Marketing Handbook is excellent.

Publications worth mentioning are the Advertising Rates and Data books. Versions of this should be available for any country or area. Contact an advertising agency for the name of your version. The Canadian Advertising Rates and Data book lists every media outlet in Canada by subject area and location: from small photocopied community newsletters to multinational publications with branches in Canada. It details what the readership is, the editorial bent, how many subscribers, so on and so forth. And it does the same for every radio and television station in the country. This resource may also be available at libraries, journalism program offices and may be bought at some expense from its publishers. Most universities, large companies and places that deal with advertising will have a copy. Although originally expensive, an agency will often give you an out-of-date copy or the publisher will happily send you a sample of last year's version for free if you write and ask.

There are several reference sources around to help you find a supplier of specific products or services. Thomas Register is a US publication that lists what seems like most companies in the United States by product. It is in every public library, all university libraries and most large company purchasing departments. Their web site lets you have access to their database as an individual for free (http://www.thomasregister.com:8000/home.html). The Canadian version is Fraser's Directory of Canadian Trade. Thomas is some 30 hard bound volumes and costs about $275.00 a year. Because it is an annual, one can often get last year's set for $25.00 or so from someone who replaces it annually. Re member that if you just want a small amount of information you can call the reference desk of most libraries and they will willingly do the work of finding it for you. Librarians are actually fulfilled by this kind of thing, and it is not an imposition to ask them to find information for you. Check out photographic, and arts and crafts magazines for more of these kind of addresses.

Sunset Color Lab
P.O. Box 46145,
Los Angeles, California,
90046, USA

This company does slide duplication at about 35 cents per dupe for 5 and less, a very good price. Their quality is excellent and they are used by a number of artists I know who require good results. They honor personal checks in U.S. funds and the only drawback seems to be that they apparently have no telephone - which has driven a friend of mine a little crazy once trying to deal with an order in a hurry. He still uses them. When I have ordered from them they sent slides in cardboard mounts which I do not personally like. One can order plastic mounts from them. Juries for shows sometimes request cardboard mounts.

Visual Horizons
180 Metro Park
Rochester, New York
14623-2666, USA,
(716)-424-5300          Fax: 716-424-5313

Multiplex Display Fixture Company
1555 Larkin Williams Road
Fenton, MO,
63026-3008 USA
(800)-325-3350

Once you have slides you will need to store them, ship them and label them. These two companies are among many that offer supplies and equipment for this. While Visual Horizons's slide duplication services are not cheap, their catalog has a very wide range of slide handling, labeling, storing and presentation options. Multiplex has slide handling, shipping and storage options as well as Polaroid printers for slides and text printers for slide mounts. Both are good starting points for this type of information.

Photolabels (USA) Inc.
419 Eisenhower Lane South
Lombard, Ill,
60148, USA
(800)-323-0776          (708)-691-8181

This company has its main branch in England and started a US operation a number of years ago. The produce photolabels from color negatives. These photographs are printed on a plastic sheet material that when peeled off the backing will literally stick to anything and not come off. The sizes are 39 x 26 mm, 50 x 39 mm, 81 x 54 mm, and 121 x 81 mm (postcard size). Quality is good and the turn-around time is supposed to be 72 hours. If you send them a slide an internegative is made for about $10.00 and that is used. In practice I have found less control with this method. Graphics and text can be added to the images with a charge. Color proofing is $25.00. Their minimum orders are very low: 25 in the larger sizes and 50 in the smaller. Prices range from about 16 cents and up in the smaller sizes and 23 cents and more for the larger ones.

These are extremely useful for small runs of catalogues, for illustrations and for packaging. The larger sizes are better quality than postcards and about as cheap (for smaller numbers) without the need for a large run. I have used them at craft shows in the small sizes as a kind of instant jewelry with a picture of my work on it. These were slapped on customers who carried them with them and when asked where they came from could direct visitors to me. I currently use them as illustrations for technical papers that I sell.

Banana Productions,
Box 2480
Sechelt, BC,
Canada V0N 3A0
(604) 885-7156        Fax: 604-885-7183

This company is run by a woman named Anna Banana whose business card says "A company with a Peel." They provide several services such as a subscription to an inexpensive mail art newsletter which lists mail art competitions and exhibitions internationally. Their unique specialty is postage stamps of one's images and for postage stamp aficionados they are done properly with perfect little round holes between the stamps. This last means little to me but is apparently very meaningful for those who are into it. Prices are good, at about $140 (Canadian funds) for 500 stamps and if one asks one gets a wonderful assortment of sample stamps. If you send 2 images the price is $260. for 500 of each. 500 copies of a block of 3 is $385; 1000 is $590. For a block of 6, prices are $625/500 and $875/1000; for a block of 9, $800/500 and $1000/1000. I've heard of at least one graduating art school class doing their poster as a sheet of stamps, one image per person. One could of course tear individual stamps off and use them. One can include text on the original sent in to be made into stamps.

### Postcards

I have found postcards a unique and very effective tool for the promotion of my work and myself. They have the advantage of serving easily as exhibition announcements and a type of permanent image-spreading tool if the picture chosen is good enough to go up on a studio or store wall. It is important to choose an image which will not be discarded; one which is interesting enough to be retained by the recipient. This means good photography and understanding that the point of the card is the image on it and not necessarily the object depicted. When post cards are given away people send them out for you, usually contacting other people who might be interested in your work. They can also often be sold through public art gallery gift shops and as it in the interest of the shop to display them prominently and sell them one gets a lot of mileage from them. At a unit cost of less than 10 cents each and with other people mailing and distributing them for you they can work well towards establishing a position in the culture. A hint: put at the very least your phone number on the back.

There are many companies that print postcards and an inexpensive local method of obtaining them is to do a 'gang run' with a group of colleagues. Usually this requires at least 8 cards (sometimes 16) done at once to obtain a discount. I am referring here to color cards as black and white do not do justice to work and are too easily discarded. If you pick an image that has a gray or mid-toned background and is not too contrasty this often improves results when a postcard is done as part of a gang run. Note that a color image of your work (even a poor one) has a peculiar kind of validity to it which a black and white print or a photocopied article on it does not possess. Photography galleries and arts and craft organizations often have an interest in organizing such gang runs. I believe that postcard production is an excellent way of gently flooding the culture with artwork and raising the profile of the arts. One can set up multiple images on the same card. Cited here are companies that produce images at reasonable prices.

ADFACTOR
982 Queen St. West
Toronto, Ontario,
Canada M6J 1H1
(416) 531-7907

ADFACTOR prints postcards at about $395 for 2500 cards with text on the back and an automatic 'bleed' (when the image runs to the edge of the card surface). Their turn-around time is about 4-6 weeks; standard in the printing industry. Any variations from their format incur added (and high) costs. One can request a color proof at added cost. They use a 4" x 6" non-glossy color print and cards are 'ganged' with 10 other ones so lower or higher numbered runs incur higher costs. One can, however, buy multiple spaces in the run and so print catalogues or combination images.

Alberta Crafts Council  (Postcard project),
10106 - 124 St.,
Edmonton, Alberta,
Canada  T5N 1P6,
(403)-488-6611

This project consists of a managed gang run at a great price of $250.00 Can. for 2500 cards. If you are not a member of the crafts council the run costs $280.00 (this is a very approximate $220.00 in US funds). This is absolutely the best Canadian (or US) price I've seen for color cards from a 35 mm slide. They will do a run anytime they have 16 people lined up so unless you want a lot of postcards done for yourself you may have to convince some other people they really need postcards or wait a little while. They have done my last five or six cards and I am very happy with the quality.

Patrick Grace Photo
P O Box 145,
York Harbor, Maine,
03911-0145, USA
(207) 363-4665

Though more expensive than the Alberta Crafts Council when I want best quality for lowest price from another source so far he is my favorite. The cards are done from a 35 mm slide which I feel allows better color reproduction without using a color proof and its added cost. Prices are currently about (US funds) $280/500; $300/1000; $365/2500; $425/5000 (including shipping). The amount of text used is limited without incurring extra costs but it is certainly adequate. Service and quality is in my opinion very good-rush printing is possible at a slight extra cost. The printing is done in Florida at Dyna-Color Co. which actually charges more than Patrick Grace to do the same thing. While he deals with many commercial cards for motels and so on, he has an ever-increasing number of artists using his services and therefore has some pressure to keep quality up. He also does 4-color business cards as low as 3 cents each and offers other printing services. I have used him six times and will again. He is very good in paper quality, printing and color trueness to the slide image sent.

Modern Postcards
1-800-959-8365 (USA only)

Modern Postcards offers 500 postcards for $95.00. While I think that this is not enough images for the effort involved in having them done the price is low enough to encourage people to start creating postcards. I have not used them but the quality I've seen is very good.

Seattle Film works,
1260-16th Ave. W.,
P O Box 34056,
Seattle, Washington
98124-9956, USA
(206) 283-9074

This company has a good reputation for slide services. They also offer slide, photo and negative digitization and manipulation (scanning, repair and changing) services. They apparently offer free 'Photo Works' floppy disks that you can show and print from your computer. They send free film back with each processing. I have not used them personally.

Paté Poste Adcards
43 Charles Street,
Boston, Massachusetts
02114 USA
Tel: (617) 720-2855      Fax: 617-723-7683

They use a color 35 mm slide or larger transparency. A number of different qualities and sizes of cards are offered and there is no extra charge for a white border or a bleed. Their basic price is about (US funds) $405/500; $432/1000; $486/2500; $567/5000; $738/10 000; $904/ 15 000; $1251/ 25 000; $2038/50 000 cards. These are the 'express' prices, for work done in 10 business days; if you can wait 5 more days, the price drops by 10 percent. The quality seems to be quite high although I have not used them myself.

Color Q
2710 Dryden Road,
Dayton, Ohio,
45439, USA
(800)-999-1007

This company has a very impressive sample pack and price list. Their postcards are available in a wide range of surfaces, acid-free papers, textures, quantities and typefaces. Examples are (for 3 1/2" x 5 1/2") 300/$170, 500/$190, 1000/$240, 2000/$300, 3000/$360. They specialize in marketing tools for 2-D artists and offer art marketing tips, posters, books and seminars as well as numerous printing options for artists such as short run introduction brochures. The person who recommended them to me praised their service and willingness to work towards a best image. Hmm, they sound pretty good. Haven't tried them yet but will at some point.

New World Books
2 Canes Road,
PO Box 89,
Suffern, New York,
10901 USA,
(914)-354-2600

New World Books offers discounts of 10-30% on books ordered. Any book in print in North America can be had from them. Several users have told me what they paid for books through this company and the prices are often what a bookstore will pay wholesale. The process of ordering and getting the book takes about six weeks.

I hope that this section has proven interesting - good luck in your PR and in raising the level of professionalism in your field. There are of course many similar useful addresses around and if you have one that you think would be good to pass on I would appreciate receiving it. Some other sources to consider that I have not reviewed here are given in the appendix.

# Check Lists

**Photo-Booth: nice items to have around**
lighting sources as described in the book
lots of mirrors (it is hard to have too many)
Fun-Tack®
5 or more hemostats
20 clothespins
a selection of different sizes of spring clamps
black thread
fishing line
string
silver duct tape
black duct tape
masking tape
aluminum foil
stainless steel wire (.029" is a good size)
steel blocks and chunks to lean work against
rear support rod and stand
pair of flat nose pliers
pair of round nose pliers
X-acto knife
scissors
Kodak gray cards
black permanent markers in different widths
pencil
thumb tacks
C-clamps
flat matte black and gray spray paint
Mylar® sheets
white ripstop nylon
white paper
Foam-Core®
white Styrofoam meat trays (reflector for front of camera)
silver, white and black cardboard
shooting surface options
lens tissue and cleaner
paper towel (don't use on lenses!)
claw hammer, selection of nails and brads
light dimmer system for ramping lights up and down
power bars/extension cord
bubble level

**Setting up the Camera Check list**
° Mounted so you can get at the film rewind button
° Film installed and wound on correctly
° Film type box top inserted in back of camera
° Battery checked
° ISO checked
° Lens front checked for cleaning requirements

**Copy Set-Up Check List (Collins, p 139)**
1) select a set
2) estimate size of art
3) position the lights
4) balance the illumination
5) place the art under the light
6) set the camera back parallel to the art
7) center the camera
8) frame the art and focus
9) check for problems
10) calculate the exposure
11) make the exposure
12) check the alignment of the camera

**Taking the Photo Check list**
- Review what the photo is supposed to do for you, what it is supposed to reveal about the object to the intended viewer.
- Object is a good proportion to frame.
- Composition is good.
- Object is shown to its best (most informative for the purpose) advantage (turn it around and check it at different angles and heights of camera angle through the viewfinder). Does the image do what you need it to?
- Model the lighting to best suit the object (and the degree of your dramatic intent).
- Re-check for poor composition.
- Check for odd lighting in background, holding stand parts visible, edges of shot for all the things you don't want there in the final image.
- Check for deep shadows and hot spots and adjust the lighting accordingly.
- Make the primary depth of field focus and f-stop decision.
- Accept the composition and lighting decisions.
- Take light meter reading off the center of the object.
- Swing the viewfinder around the object to check for hot spots and deep shadow metering variations, fix any problems in lighting if it is necessary.
- Take light meter reading half on the object and half on the shooting surface as a cross check.
- Make a light metering decision.
- Possibly check the metering decision with a gray card. Correct it if it feels appropriate.
- Shoot. (make a decision to bracket or not and by how much).

**Note:** a shorter version of this check list accompanies this book and can be pinned up next to your photo-booth. If you use a dry erase marker to check the boxes as you use it then it can be wiped off afterwards.

## Batch printing black and white prints

You need a darkroom, timer, enlarger, Polycontrast filters, Polycontrast F glossy RC paper probably cut to 4" x 5" in size, 50 mm lens, 8" x 10" easel, a 35 mm negative carrier for the enlarger, fresh chemicals, tongs, lots of paper towel (watch out for lint), a knowledgeable friend to steer you through it and so on. Work cleanly, drain chemicals from photographic paper carefully and switch tongs to avoid cross-contamination in the developing process, plan, lay things out and work carefully. Once you have taken a print through the printing cycle a few times and done a test strip or so to learn how, then the procedure for batch printing is:

1) Focus the negative with the enlarger set with the lens wide open, then stop it down and do a test strip with the enlarger set on f-11 or f-16.

2) Develop the test strip: one and a half minutes in the developer, 30 seconds in the stop, 1 minute in the fix before you can take it outside to look at it under normal lighting conditions. Then choose an exposure time.

3) Expose one piece of paper and take it through the developing process, fix it for a minute and a half and take it outside the darkroom to check it.

4) If it is good then expose 6 to 7 more sheets at the same exposure. Each sheet of paper comes out of the black plastic bag one at a time and after exposure is placed face down in a dark spot or into an envelope.

5) When done put the next negative in the negative carrier, remove all dust, focus it with the enlarger set with the lens wide open, then stop it down and do a test strip with the enlarger set on f-11 or f-16.

6) When you put the test strip in to develop it add the 6 or 7 exposed, undeveloped prints quickly making sure that they are rapidly wet. Agitate constantly through the process. When you get to the end take the test strip outside to look at it and then continue, overlapping the developing of the test strip with the developing of the previous bunch of exposed sheets.

# Appendices

## Some Sources:
Small Parts Inc., P.O. Box 4650, Miami Lakes, FL 33014, USA (stainless steel hard drawn wire, they sell a sample pack of twenty-five feet each of nine different sizes of stainless steel wire for about $14.00)

Hanneman Gemological Instruments, PO box 942L, Poulsbo, WA, 98370, USA (a source for fiber-optic lights)

GIA, 1660 Stewart Street, Santa Monica, CA, 90404, USA, Tel: 310-829-2991 (a source for fiber-optic lights)

*Small Business Reports,* PO Box 53140, Boulder, Co., 80322-3140, USA (serious information for business, I also recommend Inc. Magazine).

*The Guerrilla Marketing Handbook,* Jay Levinson and Seth Godin, Houghton Mifflin company, Boston, New York, ISBN 0-395-70013-2, ©1994 (the best of the series)

### *Some additional useful PR tool addresses*
The Slide Printer, PO Box 9506V, Denver, CO, 80209, USA (prints from slides as low as $5.00 for an 8" x 12" print)

Perma SAF, Box 320, Denville, NJ, 07834, USA (polypropylene slide pages)

Kimac Company, 478 Longhill Road, Guilford, CT, 06434, USA (archival slide protectors, Meltzer, p 108)

Kia Photography, 453 CR Main, Nashua, NH, 03060, USA

Show and Tell Communications, Dept. CR PO Box 1209, Merchantville, NJ, 08109, USA

Pelland Advertising, PO Box 878, Springfield, Mass, 01101, USA

S & M Processing, S & M House, 287 Rayne Road, Braintree, Essex CM7 7PX, England (parent company of Photolabels USA)

Dynacolor Graphics Inc., 1182 NW 159th Drive, Miami, Florida, 33169, USA

Art Editions, PO Box 2619, Salt Lake City, Utah, 84110-2619, USA

Sharon, Jerry Anthony Photography, 614-267-8909, USA

MWM Dexter Inc., PO Box 261, Aurora, MO, 65605-0261, USA

Thayer Productions, PO Box 459, Belmont, MA, 02178, USA

## Bibliography

Bomback, Edward S. *Manual of Photographic Lighting.* Kings Langley, Herts., UK: Fountain Press - Argus Books, 1971.

Collins, Sheldan, *How to Photograph Works of Art.* New York: Amphoto/Watson-Guptill, 1992

Keppler, Herbert. *The Asahi Pentax Way: The Asahi Pentax Photographer's Companion.* 9th ed. London: Focal Press, 1975.

Meltzer, Steve. *Photographing Your Craftwork: A Hands-On Guide for Craftspeople.* Crafts Report Books. Seattle: Madrona, 1986.

*Popular Photography* [SSN 0032-4582]. Diamandis Communications: P.O. Box 54912, Boulder, CO 80322-4912 USA.

Snyder, Norman, et al, eds. *The Photography Catalog.* New York: Harper and Row, 1976.

Zielke, Mon Hans, and Franklin G. Beezley. *How to Take Industrial Photographs.* New York: McGraw-Hill, 1948.

## Some URL's for Net Surfers

http://www.cmpsolv.com/los/links.html
A listing of photographers resources

http://www.users.interport.net/~sr/photo.sites.html
Lots more photo resources

http://www.best.com/~cgd/home/pholinks.htm
Over 600 photography links updated weekly.

gopher://atlas.chem.utah.edu/11/MSDS
Check the chemicals you work with at this MSDS site.

http://www.thomasregister.com:8000/home.html
Thomas Register, a great service and company finding site.

http://www.craftsreport.com/
The Crafts Report Magazine site-good stuff for networking.

http://www.xensei.com/users/adl/
The Art Deadlines list - good for competitions, exhibitions etc.

http://www.ganoksin.com/kosana/brain/brain.htm
Brain Press home page at Ganoksin.com, Lewton-Brain bio, books and video descriptions. Check out the "Tips from the Jeweler's Bench" section for numerous articles by Charles.

To send Email to Charles: brainnet@cadvision.com

**Brain Press Publications**

This list describes monographs for sale which detail the results of my research in various directions. As titles at the $15.50 retail price range are revised and updated their prices are subject to change. Binding is on the primitive side: acetate covers and plastic slides. Shipping is extra. Current titles:

**Forming using Metal Characteristics: Fold Forming** Fold forming is a system of sheet metal forming which emphasizes forming using the metal's characteristics. Forms are derived from the natural plasticity, ductility and elasticity of the metal. The system is internationally recognized as a new approach to working metal. It is extremely efficient and rapid. Tools are simple: fingers, hands, hammers, mallets, anvil and rolling mills. The paper has a theoretical introduction and step-by-step recipes for quickly working sheet metal. 45 pages, over 70 B/W line drawings. 1985/90© $15.50

**Fold Forming Video** This half-hour video serves to introduce fold-forming as a system. Made in 1986, it covers the basic folds of the system and includes a set of notes on developments since 1985. $23.50

**Patinas for Small Studios** This paper describes safer, easy patination methods for metals that involve easily obtainable and kitchen chemicals to produce blues, greens, browns, blacks, grays and reddish tones on metals. Application methods and options for pattern and surface control are described. 34 pages, 5 color pictures, 1985© $15.50

**Gold Surface Applications: A Technology Review**. The results of a research project for the Society of North American Goldsmiths. It describes fusion applications (gold painting), doublée, Keum-boo, depletion gilding (tumbaga, guanin), inlay and overlay procedures and has a discussion of fire gilding. Control factors for free compositional choice are defined and demonstrated. 27 pages. B/W diagrams, one color picture. 1985© $15.50

**Depletion Gilding: a historical and technical introduction**. It describes the approaches that goldsmiths have used historically in various cultures to remove base metals from gold alloys for refining or "coloring the gold": depletion gilding. There is an extensive listing of recipes from many historical and contemporary sources designed to foster contrast and comparison to deepen understanding of the subject. This paper is intended for information only and is not a "how to" for depletion gilding. 20 pages. 1990© $15.50

**Shareware Book:** This wide ranging, truly eclectic book is chock full of sources, suppliers, technical information, patinas, stonesetting, bench tools and thoughts on metalsmithing. About 175 pages and lots of diagrams. This is also used as a handout for Brain Press workshops. $24.95

**Cheap Thrills in the Toolshop** This is a loose, eclectic collection of short cuts, bench tricks and alternative equipment options for goldsmiths. Cheap tool making, tool conversions and unexpected sources for tools are all described. Sections include shop machines, tools, setting tools, soldering and more. Lots of drawings, lists and reviews of sources round out the book. A good index and table of contents make finding information easy. 80 pages crammed full of information. 82 line drawings. 1996© $24.95

**Brain Press**, Box 1624, Ste M, Calgary, Alberta, T2P 2L7

(403)-263-3955 , fax: 403-283-9053, Email: brainnet@cadvision.com

## Index

## *Charles Lewton-Brain*

Charles Lewton-Brain has been taking photographs of his own jewelry, sculpture and other people's work for over 20 years. He studied and worked in Germany, Canada and the United States to learn metalsmithing and goldsmithing. Some of his work is linked with performance art. The metalworking is concerned with process and beauty as well as with issues of function and non-function. Much of the jewelry uses a 'printmaking' approach to working metal, that is that the work is done in separate steps in groups building towards the finished piece. His work and writing on the results of his technical research has been published internationally. In 1991 with his partner Dee Fontans he started a resource centre and workshop school in downtown Calgary called the Lewton-Brain/Fontans Centre for Jewellery Studies which educates metal smiths. In 1994 Brain Press was established which documents, publishes and markets the results of his research activities. 1996 brought the establishment of a Brain Press collaborative web site in Thailand with Ganoksin.com.

A distinguished Fellow of the Society of North American Goldsmiths and a Fellow of the Gemmological Association of Great Britain he has lectured and taught in England, the United States, Canada and Australia. He regularly teaches workshops in the results of his research projects across North America. Charles developed 'fold forming', a series of techniques new to the metalsmithing field which allow rapid development of three dimensional surfaces and structures using simple equipment. The Rolex Awards for Enterprise chose a project of his on the further development of fold forming for inclusion in a book on innovative developments in science and invention in the world, the *Rolex Awards for Enterprise 1991 Edition.*

He has lived in Calgary since 1986 and currently teaches at the Alberta College of Art and Design as well as writing articles, exhibiting, consulting and making artwork and jewelry.